The Tenure-Track Process for Chicana and Latina Faculty

This anthology addresses the role of postsecondary institutional structures and policy in shaping the tenure-track process for Chicana and Latina faculty in higher education. Each chapter offers first-person narratives of survival in the academy employing critical theoretical contributions and qualitative empirical research. Major topics included are the importance of early socialization, intergenerational mentorship, culturally relevant faculty programming, and institutional challenges and support structures. The aim of this volume is to highlight practical and policy implications and interventions for scholars, academics, and institutions to facilitate tenure and promotion for women faculty of color.

Patricia A. Pérez, PhD, is Professor of Chicana/o Studies at California State University, Fullerton, USA.

Routledge Research in Higher Education

Virtue and the Quiet Art of Scholarship
Reclaiming the University
Anne Pirrie

Global Perspectives on International Student Experiences in Higher Education Trends and Issues
Edited by Krishna Bista

Data for Continuous Programmatic Improvement
Steps Colleges of Education Must Take to Become a Data Culture
Edited by Ellen B. Mandinach and Edith S. Gummer

Grounding Education in the Environmental Humanities
Exploring Place-Based Pedagogies in the South
Edited by Lucas F. Johnston and Dave Aftandilian

Success Factors for Minorities in Engineering
Jacqueline Fleming and Irving Pressley McPhail

Exploring Institutional Logics in Technology-Mediated Higher Education
Neelam Dwivedi

The Phenomenological Heart of Teaching and Learning
Theory, Research, and Practice in Higher Education
Katherine H. Greenberg, Brian K. Sohn, Neil B. Greenberg, Howard R. Pollio, Sandra P. Thomas, and John T. Smith

The Tenure-Track Process for Chicana and Latina Faculty
Experiences of Resisting and Persisting in the Academy
Edited by Patricia A. Pérez

For more information about this series, please visit: www.routledge.com/Routledge-Research-in-Higher-Education/book-series/RRHE

The Tenure-Track Process for Chicana and Latina Faculty
Experiences of Resisting and Persisting in the Academy

Edited by Patricia A. Pérez, PhD

NEW YORK AND LONDON

First published 2019
by Routledge
52 Vanderbilt Avenue, New York, NY 10017

and by Routledge
2 Park Square, Milton Park, Abingdon, Oxon, OX14 4RN

First issued in paperback 2020

Routledge is an imprint of the Taylor & Francis Group, an informa business

© 2019 Taylor & Francis

The right of Patricia A. Pérez to be identified as editor of this work has been asserted by her in accordance with sections 77 and 78 of the Copyright, Designs and Patents Act 1988.

All rights reserved. No part of this book may be reprinted or reproduced or utilised in any form or by any electronic, mechanical, or other means, now known or hereafter invented, including photocopying and recording, or in any information storage or retrieval system, without permission in writing from the publishers.

Trademark notice: Product or corporate names may be trademarks or registered trademarks, and are used only for identification and explanation without intent to infringe.

Library of Congress Cataloguing-in-Publication Data
A catalog record for this book has been requested

ISBN 13: 978-0-367-67070-2 (pbk)
ISBN 13: 978-0-367-22581-0 (hbk)

Typeset in Sabon
by Apex CoVantage, LLC

To my loves, Matías, Andrés, and Luna

To one of my first teachers, my nana, Refugio "Ruth" Juarez García (October 1, 1927–December 25, 2018)

Contents

Foreword ix
CAROLINE S. TURNER

Acknowledgments xiii

1 Introduction and Overview: Chicana and Latina
   Warriors in Academia 1
   PATRICIA A. PÉREZ

2 Latinas Finding Voice and Community in Academe:
   Mentoring, Socialization, and Resistance Across Generations 11
   MARICELA OLIVA AND LUCINDA NEVAREZ

3 "In Academia, But Not of It"—Redefining What It
   Means to Serve 31
   JUDY MARQUEZ KIYAMA AND LESLIE GONZALES

4 Developing Intentionality: How Postsecondary
   Institutions Can Nurture Latina Faculty Members to
   Achieve Tenure and Promotion 44
   EDLYN PEÑA

5 Reflections on Becoming a Full Professor: A Journey
   Best Walked Together 56
   JULIE LÓPEZ FIGUEROA

6 M(other)work as Radical Resurgence: Nurturing
   Survivance for Women of Color Faculty 73
   VERÓNICA N. VÉLEZ AND ANNA LEES

7 Triunfos y Tribulaciones/Triumphs and Challenges: An Intersectional Discussion on Chicana Leadership in the Academy 90
MARISELA R. CHÁVEZ, CRISTINA HERRERA, AND PATRICIA A. PÉREZ

8 Latina Administrators Practicing Resonant Leadership in the Borderlands 106
PATRICIA ARREDONDO

9 Conclusion: In Solidarity With the Community We Serve 130
MARIA ESTELA ZARATE

List of Contributors 141
Index 146

Foreword

I am honored to have this opportunity to write the foreword for this outstanding and distinctive book, *The Tenure-Track Process for Chicana and Latina Faculty: Experiences of Resisting and Persisting in the Academy*. This work is a critically important contribution to the sparse literature focusing on the lived experiences of faculty who are gravely underrepresented at each academic rank throughout higher education, Chicana and Latina faculty.

Dr. Patricia A. Pérez, a highly esteemed and productive professor and chair, provides a needed platform for distinguished Chicana/Latina scholars to tell their truth as they continue to make important contributions to higher education within various institutional contexts. The editor and chapter authors contribute critical scholarship and leadership to their respective fields and disciplines. Each is an accomplished researcher who also provides the reader with descriptions of on-the-ground experiences as she transitions into, perseveres, and grows within her work environment. Generally authors describe these environments as unwelcoming, hostile, and, at times, physically and psychologically unsafe.

In the face of adverse environments, authors underscore creating space for themselves, mentoring, networking, and providing self-care as elements conducive to their resilience and growing confidence to resist and persist in the academy. The authors also provide suggestions by which organizational intentionality and interventions can improve adverse environments toward the creation of inclusive, welcoming spaces.

With the aim of stimulating dialogue and change, this book brings to the forefront issues that many find uncomfortable talking about in academia associated with the experiences of Chicana/Latina faculty in higher education. Narratives presented here describe challenges and opportunities related to teaching, research, service, mentoring, collegiality, promotion and tenure, leadership, succession planning, as well as bullying, sexism, and racism.

This publication clearly and expertly addresses the tension between being in the minority and an outsider on the margin and retaining one's voice, rooted in personal history and values, while successfully navigating her academic environment. Through interviews with faculty of color, prior research findings indicate that "Although doctoral student and faculty socialization processes are very strong, we must not lose ourselves in the process of fitting in . . ." (Turner, 2017, p. 3). The ideas of incorporation and marginalization in the academy give rise to these emerging tensions (Turner, 2003). Such tension and how authors navigate it is reflected in the title of this book, resisting and persisting, and in the narratives presented. For example, Kiyama and Gonzales address being "in academia, but not of it," López Figueroa speaks about resisting the status quo while "hanging on to who you are and all that you bring." Vélez and Lees present the idea of "work within the university but not become of the university." Thus, this volume provides essential insights for others engaged in similar struggles and for those attempting to mitigate and remedy this circumstance.

Reaching out to Chicanas and Latinas aspiring to the professoriate and the possible leadership roles emerging from these faculty positions, this book provides essential observations, reflections, and strategies that will facilitate their retention, promotion, and career advancement. In addition, by providing detailed narratives with real-life examples, this book provides encouragement, stimulation, and support not only those beginning their academic journey but also, and just as needed, energizes those Chicanas and Latinas who have walked/are walking on similar paths.

I saw my story as a Latina/Filipina reflected in the narratives of several of the authors featured in this book. Briefly my life journey has taken me from working as a farm laborer in Hollister, California, to becoming the first in my family to go to college, to having the opportunity to serve for over thirty-plus years as a professor of education at the University of Minnesota–Twin Cities, Arizona State University–Tempe, and now California State University, Sacramento, where I was named interim dean of the College of Education. During this time, I was also elected to serve as president of the Association for the Study of Higher Education (ASHE).

Graduate students, faculty, and academic administrators come up to me and say that my work provides validation and support for the work in which they are engaged. Many of my graduate students say I am the first and only woman of color they have had as a professor and were encouraged to pursue their careers due to my teachings and research. Several scholars of color, now highly respected professors and leaders in higher education, inform me that they better understood their experience in academe as a result of reading my publications, such as *A Guest in Someone Else's House: Students of Color on Campus* (Turner, 1994). These interactions reenergize me when I feel stressed or disheartened.

Likewise, I am inspired by the many students, faculty, and administrators I have interviewed for my research on faculty diversity (Turner, 1994, 2007; Turner and González, 2014; Turner and Myers, 2000). I am grateful for all of these experiences. That said, however, transitions have always been a challenge for me, and I resonate with the peaks and valleys described in this book. I speak about these challenges and opportunities in my Association for the Study of Higher Education (ASHE) presidential address, *Lessons from the Field: Cultivating Nurturing Environments in Higher Education*, and in other publications and presentations (Turner, 2015, 2017, 2018). As in this book, I use story in my work. I acknowledge and am buoyed by those researchers who support the narrative approach as legitimate scholarship and encourage its use as important sources of knowledge of the human experience.

Reading the narratives in this text, I found myself applauding all the contributions and accomplishments described, while at other times I found myself saddened and disappointed by the seemingly intractable challenges chronicled. As I finished the final chapter, I can say that this book has a revitalizing effect on me, as each chapter author(s) provides insight, encouragement, and stimulation to continue my own work.

In a previous publication, *Pathways to the Presidency: Biographical Sketches of Women of Color Firsts*, I state the following:

> Firsts pave the way for others to follow. They have no like models to emulate or like peers to mentor them. They explore new vistas and create new horizons. . . . Women who are the first of their gender and their race and ethnicity in presidential roles are torchbearers imparting knowledge and inspiration to others.
> (Turner, 2007, p. 32)

The editor and authors of chapters featured in this book include Chicanas/Latinas who are first in their family to attend college and the first to occupy leadership and senior faculty positions in their departments, colleges, and so on. As firsts, they are also torchbearers who create new knowledge and new horizons. In conclusion, this book makes an immense contribution toward understanding how one can support and uplift the current as well as the next generation of Chicana/Latina scholars. The narratives of these Chicana/Latina faculty leaders demonstrate how they work to actively contribute to as well as to change the academic landscape in higher education for the successful recruitment, retention, and development of future Chicana/Latina scholars, academic administrators, and campus leaders.

Caroline S. Turner, PhD
California State University, Sacramento

References

Turner, C. (2018). *Invited keynote address at the University of California, Davis (UCD) school of education graduation ceremony.* Retrieved June 13th from. https://video.ucdavis.edu/media/2018+School+of+Education+Keynote+-+Carolyn+Turner+-+June+13%2C+2018/0_g94khb64

Turner, C. S. (1994). A guest in someone else's house: Students of color on campus. *The Review of Higher Education, 17*(4), 355–370.

Turner, C. S. (2003). Incorporation and marginalization in the academy: From border toward center for faculty of color? *Journal of Black Studies, 34*(1), 112–125.

Turner, C. S. (2007). Pathways to the presidency: Biographical sketches of women of color firsts. *Harvard Educational Review, 77*(1), 1–38.

Turner, C. S. (2015). Lessons from the field: Cultivating nurturing environments in higher education. *Review of Higher Education, 38*(3), 333–358.

Turner, C. S. V. (2017). Remaining at the margin and in the center. *Journal for the Study of Postsecondary and Tertiary Education, 2,* 121–126. Retrieved from https://doi.org/10.28945/3886

Turner, C. S. V., and González, J. C. (Eds.). (2014). *Modeling mentoring across race/ethnicity and gender: Practices to cultivate the next generation of diverse faculty.* Sterling, VA: Stylus Publishing, LLC.

Turner, C. S. V., and Myers, Jr. S. L. (2000). *Faculty of color in academe: Bittersweet success.* Needham Heights, MA: Allyn and Bacon.

Acknowledgments

I would like to thank my first educators and mentors who shaped and guided my person and value system, my parents, Angelita and Javier Pérez, and my grandparents, Refugio Juarez García and José Merced Pineda García. Only because of their sacrifice and resolve am I able to indulge in a profession where I can be of assistance to our communities. I would also like to say *gracias* to my partner, Jovan, for his support throughout all these years. A big thank you to my Chicana mastermind and my comadres, Elissa Lerma and Irene I. Vega, and my academic madrina, Julie, for sustaining me. We do not spend nearly enough time together, but when we do, it is magic! I am also tremendously grateful to the women who graciously contributed to this volume. Despite the fact that you already had full plates, you managed to squeeze another project into your agendas. I truly am privileged to know, interact with, and learn from your brilliance. You have no idea how much your previous work and these chapters have inspired me! Finally I am especially humbled and appreciative to have Caroline S. Turner, PhD, contribute the foreword to this volume. I could not think of a better individual to initiate this ongoing and critical dialogue.

1 Introduction and Overview
Chicana and Latina Warriors in Academia

Patricia A. Pérez

While the number of Latino students has increased in postsecondary institutions across the U.S., the number of Chicano and Latino faculty has not increased at the same rate, despite evidence documenting the importance of a faculty body reflecting its student demographic to facilitating student retention and academic success (Musu-Gillette et al., 2017). Data reveal that while approximately 28 percent of students in U.S. postsecondary institutions are Latino, the majority of which are female, only 4 percent of all faculty reflect the same ethnic group (Ponjuan, 2011). Further, when reviewing the stratification of Chicano and Latino faculty across the professoriate relative to their white counterparts, statistics make evident they are less likely to be tenured and promoted (Hernandez, Murakami, and Rodriguez, 2015). A closer look reveals that women of color faculty fare worse, with fewer and fewer to be found (amongst a select group to begin with) in each subsequent academic rank (Social Sciences Feminist Network Research Interest Group, 2017; Ryu, 2010). To be specific, National Center for Education Statistics (NCES) data outline that Chicana and Latina lecturers, instructors, assistant professors, associate professors, and full professors account for 4 percent, 4 percent, 3 percent, 3 percent, and less than 1 percent, respectively, of all full-time faculty (U.S. DOE, NCES, 2018). American Indian female faculty constitute 1 percent or less of the total full-time faculty in each rank. African American female faculty account for 3 percent, 5 percent, 4 percent, 3 percent, and 2 percent, of lecturers, instructors, assistant professors, associate professors, and full professors, respectively. Meanwhile Asian/Pacific Islander female lecturers, instructors, assistant professors, associate professors, and full professors make up 4 percent, 3 percent, 6 percent, 5 percent, and 3 percent, respectively, of full-time faculty. These statistics are relative to 55 percent and 27 percent of full-time white male and female full professors, or 36 percent and 44 percent of white male and female lecturers (U.S. DOE, NCES, 2018). What can postsecondary institutions do to improve these figures? How can we improve institutional structures and policy to support Chicana and Latina faculty and other women of color through each academic rank? How, when, and what do model structures and policies look like when enacted?

Consonant with Whitaker and Grollman (2019) and Gutiérrez y Muhs, Flores Niemann, González, and Harris (2012) but with a more tailored focus, in this edited volume, Chicana and Latina faculty, administrators, and a former president share their narratives of resistance and persistence in successfully navigating the tenure and promotion process. In particular, each chapter offers a first-person or composite narrative of survival in the academy employing critical and asset-based theoretical contributions and qualitative research. Each chapter concludes with important implications for policy and practice. Specifically major topics addressed in this edited volume include the importance of early socialization, intergenerational mentorship, culturally relevant faculty development and programming, and intentionality within institutional challenges and support structures. More importantly, the primary goal of this edited volume is to gain a better understanding of how Chicana and Latina faculty participate in (or are engaged by) the tenure-track process to highlight pragmatic intervention strategies and practical and policy implications to facilitate tenure and promotion for women faculty of color. Consequently, through the successful tenure and promotion of more women of color, racially and ethnically diverse students they interact with, as well as their colleagues, will also benefit. This text will be of interest to scholars, policymakers, and institutions committed to increasing and supporting faculty diversity across all academic ranks of higher education.

In the first part of this chapter, I share a vignette that highlights the significance of this text as well as one of the impetuses for this book. In the next section, I offer a brief literature review that previews some of the major themes discussed throughout the larger text. The final section addresses how this text is organized.

Impetus of This Book

In my second year on the tenure track, I attended an awards ceremony for faculty colleagues. I was visibly pregnant with my first child and standing with some of my department colleagues with a white male administrator after the ceremony. The administrator pointed at my stomach, looked at my department colleague, and asked if my department colleague who happened to be standing next to me, who happened to be standing next to his partner, fathered my child.

The administrator knew that we were from the same department. After all, he had approved our hires. The only reply I could think of was "no." I do not remember if I said anything else or if anyone else challenged the remark, but I do remember the subject changed soon thereafter. I was caught off guard, embarrassed, and stunned. What did this administrator think we were up to in our department? His inappropriate comment was rooted in a gendered and ethnic stereotype assigned to many Chicanas and Latinas, that of being fertile and/or baby-making machine. As Lugo-Lugo (2012) argued, "the same ideas we find in society at large operate within the confines of the university, because it is part of and develops from that very society" (p. 42).

The aforementioned anecdote is one example of the type of experiences I was not prepared for and unfortunately are all too common, as a Chicana in academia. Lamentably Chicana and Latina and other women of color faculty have experienced and shared other horrific accounts (see Gutiérrez y Muhs et al., 2012). To be certain, this work is inspired by other critical and qualitative research that centers the Chicana and Latina voice and underscores how, despite the fact that Chicanas and Latinas and other women of color in academia have been undervalued, emotionally taxed, ill-compensated, under-mentored, and overburdened, we remain fierce leaders, change agents, and warriors (Cuádraz, 2005; Cueva, 2013; Lopez, 2013; Medina and Luna, 2000; Turner, González, and Wong (Lau), 2011; Turner, González, and Wood, 2008; Ramos, 2008).

This text was created with the hope of supporting future and current Chicana, Latina, and other women of color faculty going through the tenure-track process and beyond so they may be better prepared to *handle* academia. This book is a reminder that you are not alone and the narratives offered throughout the chapters will provide guidance, assurance, space to reflect, and strategies to thrive.

Latinas in Academia

> We will change the academy, even as the academy changes us. And more and more of us will experience academic success – with few, if any, regrets.
> —Laura Rendón (1992, p. 63)

Over time, the research focused on Chicana and Latina students, faculty, and administrators and their experiences has increased (see, for example, Castellanos and Jones, 2003; Cuádraz, 1992, 2005; Gándara, 1982; Lopez, 2013; Medina and Luna, 2000; Turner, 2007; Turner and González, 2014). Certainly, as women started to outnumber men in higher education and the Latino demographic continued to grow, more and more important research was dedicated to these populations. Increasingly the literature has become more critical and voice-centered. Along the same vein, this text not only incorporates Chicana, Latina, and Indigenous authors, but each of the contributors employs a critical and asset-based theoretical framework. To preview some of the major themes and approaches included in this book, I provide a select review of the literature below. Each of the respective chapters will provide additional context with regard to important background literature and theoretical contributions.

While out of the scope of this text, it is important to address that a successful trajectory in academia begins before the tenure-track position commences, and preparation would take place as early as graduate school. Unfortunately seminal work by Caroline Turner and colleagues has highlighted the distinct and inequitable experiences of Chicanas and other women of color in graduate and doctoral programs (Turner, 1994; Turner and González, 2014; Turner and Thompson, 1993). For example, through interviews with thirty-seven women of color and twenty-five white women doctoral students, Turner and Thompson (1993) found:

> In general, majority women participating in this study had more opportunities than women of color for such apprenticeship opportunities as research and teaching assistantships, coauthoring papers with a faculty member, making presentations at professional conferences, and being introduced by faculty to a network of influential academics who could provide support for students seeking entry-level jobs.
>
> (p. 360)

Further, while women of color doctoral students reported "relative isolation, a lack of faculty mentoring experiences, and a lack of collegiality with other doctoral students" (p. 366), white women doctoral students reported more student- and faculty-initiated mentoring opportunities. As a result, Turner and Thompson (1993) conclude that women of color are less successful in academia because they tend to have fewer opportunities for professional socialization in graduate school, a conclusion that is eerily similar to faculty experiences on the tenure track shared by Oliva and Nevarez (this volume).

Other formative work focused on Chicanas and higher education highlights the power of Chicana and Latina scholars using lived experiences and narratives to bring awareness to speak to their truths (Cuádraz, 2005). One prime example is Berta Cueva's (2013) research, which not only centered the voices of twenty-one Chicana and Native American women in PhD programs, but also employed a critical race theory (CRT) and Chicana feminist lens coupled with the methodology of *testimonio*. Per Cuevas (2013), she used *testimonio* "as both method and methodology to preserve and document the educational experiences of Chicanas and Native American women as they navigate through the educational pipeline" (p. 54).

She further added, "Although there is no set definition of *testimonio*, it is based on accounts of lived experiences and collective solidarity against a common system of oppression" (p. 54). Among the significant contributions of her research, Cueva (2013) provides a "survival guide for students of color" gleamed from her *testimonios* focused on the following themes: internal university responses and resources; external university responses and resources; health-related responses and resources; and spiritual responses and resources. Indeed the strength and use of *testimonios* by Chicana and Latina scholars has been well documented as not only a methodology but also a pedagogy and political practice (Delgado Bernal, Burciaga, and Flores Carmona, 2018).

In *Testimonios of Latina Junior Faculty: Bridging Academic, Family, and Community Lives in the Academy*, Saldaña, Castro-Villareal, and Sosa (2013) combined a Latina/Chicana feminist and CRT of identities theories with *testimonio* as a methodology to "examine the complexity of our professional and personal identities as academics and members of families and communities to theorize our common experiences as Latina/Chicana faculty" (pp. 32). The scholars revealed that while challenges in academia have not changed, Chicana and Latina faculty continue to strategize, survive, resist, and need to continue to be their own advocates. Ultimately the authors argued:

> Chicana/Latina faculty continue to navigate cultural 'borderlands' in academia, as we struggle to carve a rightful space as scholars in our disciplines, while maintaining compromiso (or commitment) to our families, communities, and students in higher education as mothers, daughters, and activists.
>
> (p. 32)

Similarly, with a focus on Latina faculty persistence in engineering, Sanchez-Peña, Main, Sambamurthy, Cox, and McGee's (2016) literature review used intersectionality theory to highlight both challenges and strategies to retain Latina faculty. While the availability of mentors posed one of the most significant challenges, the scholars offered that mentorship was instrumental in recruiting and retaining Latina faculty in engineering. Additionally they found while balancing career and family demands proved difficult, family (both chosen and real) also served as a source of motivation (Sanchez-Peña et al., 2016).

Meanwhile, Medina and Luna (2000) analyze narratives by three Latina faculty in education using a phenomenological framework. Among their findings, the authors shared that tokenism, marginalization, isolation, and heavy teaching and service loads relative to their nonminority counterparts proved particularly challenging as they navigated their faculty roles. In a more recent qualitative inquiry, Bautista Pertuz (2017) focused on the experiences and career aspirations of midlevel, Latina, student affairs administrators using a CRT, Latino CRT, and critical race feminism analytical framework. Among the experiences discussed included the value and contributions Latinas bring to their institutions; the tokenization of being placed in diversity roles; experiences with gender, race, and ethnic microaggressions; and barriers to professional advancement.

Further, the scholar highlighted that in order for institutions to best support Latina administrators, it is important for institutions to assess their campus climates and provide welcoming environments for Latinas and other women of color. She also recommended intentional recruitment, inclusive onboarding, formal mentoring assistance, clear career pathways for upward mobility, ongoing professional development opportunities, and diversity training for all administrators in top leadership roles. Interestingly, almost a decade earlier, Medina and Luna (2000) recommended similar strategies to retain and support Latina faculty on the tenure track.

Finally Bautista Pertuz (2017) noted that in addition to fundamental Latino-targeted leadership programs, providing flexibility with regard to family obligations and work schedule (for purposes of PhD degree attainment) were also key to the promotion of Latinas to top leadership roles. Bautista Pertuz's findings are consistent with previous research on Chicanas and Latinas in administrative and other leadership roles (Bonilla-Rodriguez, 2011; Canul, 2003; Crespo, 2013; Lopez, 2013; Ramos, 2008).

Organization of the Book

Despite challenges and at times hostile academic work environments, many of us have persevered. *The Tenure-Track Process for Chicana and Latina Faculty: Experiences of Resisting and Persisting in the Academy* is about those stories of resilience and resistance as well as the strategies used to make the university work for us. It is about the types of support we draw on to maintain our integrity, morale, and self-worth as human beings in a system that was not constructed with people that look like us in mind.

Building off the literature and major themes outlined in the previous section, in the next chapter, "Latinas Finding Voice and Community in Academe: Mentoring, Socialization, and Resistance Across Generations," Drs. Maricela Oliva and Lucinda Nevarez discuss the important role of culturally responsive mentoring and supportive environments in their own tenure-track journey. Further they share recent developments in their institution's role to promote their tenure-related goals and suggestions for improvement. Chapter Three, "'In Academia, But Not of It'—Redefining What It Means to Serve," by Drs. Judy Marquez Kiyama and Leslie Gonzales, draws from their cultural and historical knowledge to discuss how they approach and redefine university service. Focusing on common experiences as family-oriented, first-generation college students growing up on ranches in the Southwest, the authors outline how their approach to service is tied to a larger vision for a more just academy.

In "Developing Intentionality: How Postsecondary Institutions Can Nurture Latina Faculty Members to Achieve Tenure and Promotion," Dr. Edlyn Peña shares her near exit from her university and the way in which her institution adapted to support her advancement and subsequent tenure and creation of a resource center. In addition, she calls for "intentionality" (Tugend, 2018) in institutional reward and support structures, coupled with honoring *familismo* (De Luca and Escoto, 2012), to promote the advancement of Latina faculty at predominantly white institutions.

In Chapter Five, "Reflections on Becoming a Full Professor: A Journey Best Walked Together," Dr. Julie López Figueroa highlights which aspects of her doctoral training best prepared her to meet the academic rigor and expectations associated with tenure. She also identifies challenges, sustainability issues, and which networking practices and mentoring opportunities successfully positioned her to strike a personal and professional balance to thrive within an often-dehumanizing academic context.

Grounded in Chicana feminist and indigenous epistemologies, in Chapter Six, Drs. Verónica N. Vélez and Anna Lees use *testimonio* (Cruz, 2012) to share their lived experiences as women faculty of color (one Chicana and one Indigenous) in tenure-track positions, while simultaneously speaking back to institutions of higher education. In "M(other) work as Radical Resurgence: Nurturing Survivance for Women of Color Faculty," the authors frame their *testimonio* in three parts: sisterhood, m(other)work as radical resurgence, and intergenerational dreams of the postcolonial.

In the following chapter by Drs. Maricela R. Chávez, Cristina Herrera, and Patricia A. Pérez, "Triunfos y Tribulaciones/Triumphs and Challenges: An Intersectional Discussion on Chicana Leadership in the Academy," the authors use the Chicana feminist concepts of *sitios y lenguas* (spaces and languages) (Pérez, 1998) to discuss both achievements and challenges as department chairs at public institutions. Based on their collective narratives, they offer practical and policy implications, including the importance of reaching out to Chicana chairs and establishing a Chicana mastermind (claiming a space), creating *confianza* (trust) and academic *comadrazgo* (academic kin), and sharing and mentorship.

Employing an appreciative inquiry approach with eight Latina leaders from department chair to president, in Chapter Eight, Dr. Patricia Arredondo shares how these leaders have thrived in predominantly white institutions. In "Latina Administrators Practicing Resonant Leadership in the Borderlands," she draws from Gloria Anzaldúa's (1987) concepts of the borderlands and *nepantla* as well as describes how women apply emotional intelligence (EI) and resonant leadership practices to be successful leaders. Among the major topics discussed in her chapter using a strength-based lens, she highlights women leaders in the academy, leadership paradigms, culture-centered approaches to inquiring and learning, and Latina leaders in action.

The final chapter, "Conclusion: In Solidarity with the Community We Serve," by Dr. Maria Estela Zarate brings together the main findings, interventions, theoretical frameworks, and practical and policy implications outlined across the previous chapters. She also provides a select list of national resources in order to nurture community and support in academia. Collectively, the chapters are central in assisting faculty and administrators and informing institutional policymakers by highlighting critical areas in need of improvement and additional resources to support Chicana and Latina faculty. This text emphasizes the need to support the retention and promotion of Chicana and Latina faculty from a multipronged approach.

It is important to acknowledge the limitations of this volume. First, while this text centers on the Chicana and Latina faculty voice, it is not exhaustive of the full diversity of Latina ethnic representation or institutional experiences. For example, Chicana and Latina community college faculty are not among the authors reflected in this text.

Second, the chapter authors included in this volume have been "successful" in the academy within institutional structures and guidelines outlined at their respective postsecondary institutions. This text does not include Chicana and Latina faculty who *earned* tenure but were not *granted* tenure. However, despite these limitations, I hope this text offers a manner by which to instigate the conversation on how best to support Chicana, Latina, and other women of color of faculty in the academy at institutions across the U.S. and beyond. As student demographics continue to change across postsecondary institutions in the U.S., the diversity of our professoriate and those in administrative roles becomes paramount and key to retaining and preparing the next generation of leaders.

References

Anzaldúa, G. (1987). *Borderlands/La Frontera: The New Mestiza*. San Francisco, CA: Aunt Lute Books.

Bautista Pertuz, S. (2017). *The chosen tokens: Exploring the work experiences and career aspirations of Latina midlevel student affairs administrators in higher education* (Unpublished doctoral dissertation). Seton Hall University, South Orange, NJ.

Bonilla-Rodriguez, D. M. (2011). *A profile of Latina leadership in the United States: Characteristics, positive influences, and barriers* (Doctoral Dissertation). St. John Fisher College, Rochester, NY.

Canul, K. H. (2003). Latina/o cultural values and the academy: Latinas navigating through the administrative role. In J. Castellanos and L. Jones (Eds.), *The majority in the minority: Expanding the representation of Latina/o faculty, administrators and students in higher education* (pp. 167–175). Sterling, VA: Stylus Publishing, LLC.

Castellanos, J., and Jones, L. (2003). *The majority in the minority: Expanding the representation of Latina/o faculty, administrators and students in higher education*. Sterling, VA: Stylus Publishing, LLC.

Crespo, N. (2013). *Latina women: How they succeed factors that influence the career advancement of Latina women in higher education* (Unpublished doctoral dissertation). University of Pennsylvania, Philadelphia, PA.

Cruz, C. (2012). Making curriculum from scratch: "Testimonio" in an urban classroom. *Equity & Excellence in Education, 45*(3), 460–471.

Cuádraz, G. H. (1992). Experiences of multiple marginality: A case of Chicana scholarship women. *Journal of the Association of Mexican American Educators, 12,* 31–43.

Cuádraz, G. H. (2005). Chicanas and higher education: Three decades of literature and thought. *Journal of Hispanic Higher Education, 4*(3), 215–234.

Cueva, B. M. (2013). *Theorizing the racial and gendered educational experiences of Chicanas and Native American women at the Ph.D. level in higher education: Testimonios of resistance, defiance, survival, and hope* (Unpublished doctoral dissertation). University of California, Los Angeles, CA.

De Luca, S. M., and Escoto, E. R. (2012). The recruitment and support of Latino faculty for tenure and promotion. *Journal of Hispanic Higher Education, 11,* 29–40.

Delgado Bernal, D., Burciaga, R., and Flores Carmona, J. (2018). *Chicana/Latina testimonies as pedagogical, methodological, and activist approaches to social justice.* New York, NY: Routledge.

Gándara, P. (1982). Passing through the eye of the needle: High-achieving Chicanas. *Hispanic Journal of Behavioral Sciences, 4*(2), 167–179.

Gutierrez y Muhs, G., Niemann, Y. F., and Gonzalez, C. G., and Harris, A. P. (Eds.). (2012). *Presumed incompetent: The intersections of race and class for women in academia.* Logan, UT: University of Utah Press.

Hernandez, F., Murakami, E., and Rodriguez, G. M. (2015). *Abriendo puertas, cerrando heridas (Opening doors, closing wounds): Latinas/os finding work-life balance in academia.* Charlotte, NC: Information Age Publishing.

Lopez, M. M. (2013). *Latina administrators' ways of leadership: Preparando Chicanas* (Unpublished doctoral dissertation). Texas A & M University, College Station, TX.

Lugo-Lugo, C. R. (2012). A prostitute, a servant, and a customer service representative: A Latina in academia. In G. Gutiérrez y Muhs, Y. Flores Niemann, C. G. González, and A. P. Harris (Eds.), *Presumed incompetent: The intersections of race and class for women in academia* (pp. 40–49). Logan, UT: Utah State University Press.

Medina, C., and Luna, G. (2000). Narratives from Latina professors in higher education. *Anthropology & Education Quarterly, 31*(1), 47–66.

Musu-Gillette, L., de Brey, C., McFarland, J., Hussar, W., Sonnenberg, W., and Wilkonson-Flicker, S. (2017). *Status and trends in the education of racial and ethnic groups 2017 (NCES 2017–051).* Washington, DC: U.S. Department of Education, National Center for Education Statistics.

Saldaña, L.P., Castro-Villareal, F., and Sosa, E. (2013, Winter-Spring). Testimonios of Latina junior faculty: Bridging academia, familia, and community lives in the academy. *Educational Foundations, 27*(1–2), 31–48.

Sanchez-Peña, M., Main, J., Sambamurthy, N., Cox, M., and McGee, E. (2016, October 12–15). *The factors affecting the persistence of Latina faculty: A literature review using the intersectionality of race, gender, and class.* Paper presented at the IEEE Frontiers in Education Conference, Erie, PA. doi:10.1109/FIE.2016.7757519

Pérez, E. (1998). Sexuality and discourse: Notes from a Chicana survivor. In C. Trujillo (Ed.), *Chicana lesbians: The girls our mothers warned us about* (pp. 159–184). Berkeley, CA: Third Woman Press.

Ponjuan, L. (2011). Recruiting and retaining Latino faculty members: The missing piece to Latino student success. *Thought and Action, 27*, 99–110.

Ramos, S. M. (2008). *Latina presidents of four-year institutions, penetrating the adobe ceiling: A critical review.* Tucson, AZ: The University of Arizona.

Rendón, L. L. (1992). From the barrio to the academy: Revelations of a Mexican American "scholarship girl." *New Directions for Colleges, 80*, 55–65.

Ryu, M. (2010). *Minorities in higher education: Twenty-fourth status report.* Washington, DC: American Council on Education.

Social Sciences Feminist Network Research Interest Group. (2017). The burden of invisible work in academia: Social inequalities and time use in five university departments. *Humboldt Journal of Social Relations, 39*(39), 228–245.

Tugend, A. (2018, June 17). How serious are you about diversity hiring? *The Chronicle of Higher Education.* Retrieved from www.chronicle.com/article/How-Serious-Are-You-About/243684

Turner, C. S. (1994). Guests in someone else's house: Students of color. *Review of Higher Education, 17*(4), 355–370.

Turner, C. S. (2007). Pathways to the presidency: Biographical sketches of women of color firsts. *Harvard Educational Review, 77*(1), 1–38.

Turner, C. S. V., and González, J. C. (2014). Walking with company! Camindo Acompañados! Mentoring Latina/o students in the 21st century. In P. F. Felder and E. P. St. John (Eds.), *Supporting graduate students in the 21st century: Implications for policy and practice. readings on equal education* (vol. 27., pp. 177–195). New York, NY: AMS Press.

Turner, C. S. V., González, J. C., and Wong (Lau), K. (2011). Faculty women of color: The critical nexus of race and gender. *Journal of Diversity in Higher Education, 4*(4), 199–211.

Turner, C. S. V., González, J. C., and Wood, J. L. (2008). Faculty of color in academe: What twenty years of literature tells us. *Journal of Diversity in Higher Education, 1*, 139–168.

Turner, C. S. V., and Thompson, J. R. (1993). Socializing women doctoral students: Minority and majority experiences. *Review of Higher Education, 16*(3), 335–370.

U.S. DOE, National Center for Education Statistics (NCES). (2018). *The Condition of Education (NCES 2018–144).* Characteristics of Postsecondary Faculty.

Whitaker, M. C., and Grollman, E. A. (2019). *Counternarratives from women of color academics: Bravery, vulnerability, and resistance.* New York, NY: Routledge.

2 Latinas Finding Voice and Community in Academe

Mentoring, Socialization, and Resistance Across Generations

Maricela Oliva and Lucinda Nevarez

As she was informally introduced to ASHE[1] conference participants by newcomer guide Berta Vigil Laden at the 1997 conference, Oliva mentioned having just received a higher education PhD (August 1997) from the department of educational administration at UT Austin. One of the new acquaintances asked, "Oh, so you are one of the ten?" Oliva asked what she meant and was told that she was one of the ten Latina PhDs in educational administration in the country that year.

Before graduating with a doctorate in higher education administration, Maricela Oliva had learned that Latinos as a group made up about 3 percent of the doctoral graduates each year in all disciplines across the country. It was also the case that the majority of doctoral graduates of Latino/Hispanic background were clustered in a few fields, including education. However, the starkly low percentages did not resonate with Maricela until hearing that in all of higher education, only ten people who graduated in 1997 were Latinas. While stunning, that still did not cause her to anticipate what that might mean for her experience as a new faculty member. As it turned out, the low representation of Latinas would have a significant professional and personal impact (Oliva, Rodriguez, Alanis, and Quijada, 2013). It showed up in how she was received (Delgado Bernal and Villalpando, 2002; Gibson, 2006), in male non-Latino faculty colleagues' lack of appreciation for and awareness of her background and identity (Gonzales, Murakami, and Núñez, 2013), what departmental colleagues expected or thought of her (Christie, 2014), and how her priorities and values often did not align with those of senior white male colleagues and so were routinely discounted or not supported (Acevedo-Gil and Madrigal-Garcia, 2018; Thompson, 2018).

It has been twenty-one years since that initial ASHE conversation. Today new Latinx faculty are told that things have changed dramatically, Latinas are graduating in larger numbers annually, and academe is a much more welcoming environment. To what extent is that the case? How much has the university environment changed vis-à-vis its knowledge of and acceptance of Latinas? How much more do universities need to do for Latinas to feel welcome and accepted (Mkandawire-Valhmu, Kako, and Stevens, 2010; Zambrana et al., 2015)?

In the sections that follow, two Latina academics explore these and other aspects of their experience as faculty members. The first of these, Maricela, is the 1997 doctoral graduate referenced in the opening anecdote. The second, Lucinda Nevarez, received her social work doctorate in 2010. Both now work at the same postsecondary institution, a striving Hispanic-Serving Institution (HSI) attempting to model both access and excellence within its mission.

Maricela and Lucinda recently came together through a formal institutional mentoring program that pairs tenured and new faculty members (Faurer, Sutton, and Worster, 2014; Johnson, 2007; Turner and Gonzales, 2014; Watson, Mack, and Camacho, 2012). Through the mentoring program, the two address and work through faculty development issues (Johnson, 2007). In the process, they consider their experiences in academe, including the need to develop a voice as women of color to actualize their values and academic goals. They discuss finding or developing survival strategies and mechanisms and knowledge for establishing their place within professional and disciplinary structures (Acevedo-Gil and Madrigal-Garcia, 2018; Chesney-Lind, Okamoto, and Irwin, 2006). With this mentoring engagement as a backdrop, the two explore several aspects of their experience:

- What were their early socialization and professional experiences—positive and negative—for the professoriate and work in academe?
- What is their experience with mentors or sponsors, especially those key to success in the professoriate?
- What strategies for self-empowerment and voice did they develop or use in academe?

The following section presents Maricela's journey as *antecedent*, *entry*, and *incorporation* phases. The antecedent phase identifies and captures the socializing experiences immediately prior to engaging in faculty work that shaped her academic outlook and approach for the professoriate. The entry[2] phase covers the culture clash or *choques* that Maricela encountered as a new faculty member, and finally the incorporation phase illuminates how things changed for her after successfully achieving tenure. Maricela's story will be followed by Lucinda's story and subsequently by a description that interweaves their experiences. We end with a discussion of what has changed for Latinas across a generation and what yet needs to be done to support Latinas in the professoriate.

Maricela's Story: Antecedent, Entry, and Incorporation

Antecedent

In the seven years immediately before becoming a faculty member (1990–1997) and while studying for the doctorate, Maricela worked at the

Texas state agency for higher education during a critical moment in time. Issues associated with historic racial discrimination and the marginalization of Latinos and African Americans in the formerly segregated Texas education system had, as of 1983, finally started to be addressed. The governor, state agency for higher education, and all postsecondary institutions were defendants in the *Lulac v. Richards* case (Ortegon, 2013) litigated by the Mexican American Legal Defense and Education Fund (MALDEF). MALDEF argued that because state formula funding allocated more funds for graduate and doctoral programs (of which border universities had few) than for undergraduate programs, the state was discriminating in its funding against institutions that served predominately Mexican American students. Hispanic-serving[3] universities were situated in the forty counties along the Texas-Mexico border, an area that itself had a predominately Mexican American population. MALDEF was able to show that residents in predominately white parts of the state benefitted from the availability of multiple graduate and doctoral programs in close proximity while border residents had to move or drive hundreds of miles to access programs. The inequitable distribution of programs and opportunity became apparent and widely known during the lawsuit and seemed prima facie evidence of MALDEF's argument about discrimination (Ortegon, 2013). Nonetheless, participants on both sides of the case found ample justification for their positions regarding practices within higher education and their legal merits.

During this period, in 1990 Maricela took a position for the state higher education agency to monitor Office of Civil Rights compliance in state community colleges. By 1991, she was recruited to work in the agency's executive suite by the commissioner, explicitly to help him better understand the Mexican American community point of view on issues covered in the lawsuit.

In inviting her to work as his assistant, Commissioner Ashworth explicitly asked Maricela to articulate the Mexican American perspective on issues since other white and male executive officers lacked that insight. Ashworth had discovered through experience that relying on his entirely white and male executive officers left him ill-prepared to anticipate and understand what he would hear from community members when he visited different parts of the state. In border areas like El Paso, Laredo, McAllen, and Brownsville, he might be confronted by questions or comments that he was not well prepared to address. In those exchanges, he too often found that he had not anticipated the issues that were presented to him and so was not ready with a response.

By articulating a Mexican American community perspective during internal meetings and discussion, Maricela was to help him be better prepared. Despite being relatively new to the agency and the only person among executive officers who did not already have a doctoral degree, having her speak up and express her views over several years fostered a willing outspokenness in Maricela. The responsibility to speak up as a cultural expert on litigation and other issues was initially difficult among the larger group of senior and more experienced executive officers. However, Maricela worked to overcome prior socialization as a Latina to *not* speak. By the end of her time at the agency, she was a certified mediator and had developed confidence in presenting and representing her views, even on difficult and contentious topics.

Maricela's participation and involvement in *Lulac vs. Richards* litigation helped her become well versed in macro-level state higher education and policy issues. She learned about state-specific issues that not only impacted the lawsuit and also about Adams case[4] litigation and the state's voluntary desegregation plan, both of which influenced and shaped the desegregation of Texas' higher education institutions.

During her time there, the agency and commissioner also supported her doctoral studies with leaves of absences when she requested time away to achieve important doctoral milestones. The experience and support meant that she was a different person after seven years than when she had begun. She had not only completed the PhD, she had acquired state agency knowledge in the context of navigating litigation and work as an in-group member of the Mexican American community and, at least initially, an out-group member of state agency leadership.

Entry

Offered the opportunity to remain at the state agency after graduation, Maricela instead chose to pursue a full-time year of data gathering, analysis, and writing after getting a dissertation project approved. She had learned that the state agency, as a creature of the legislature, could not serve a transformative role, but would always be guided by state legislative policy priorities. Furthermore, as a state agency rather than a teaching institution, it had no direct engagement with higher education students, something she felt was needed to change hearts and minds in practice.

While gathering data across North America to complete her dissertation study, Maricela also applied for open faculty positions in Texas, particularly along the Texas-Mexico border that had been the subject of *Lulac v. Richards*. After graduation, she accepted a faculty position at the University of Texas-El Paso (UTEP). As the first in her discipline of higher education to be hired there, she was given the task of developing a higher education program, which committee members and the dean said was much needed in the region.

Hired concurrently with a second assistant professor for the K-12 program, it quickly became evident to her that she was at a support disadvantage in comparison to her peer colleague. The male assistant professor was in the same K-12 field as senior faculty, white like senior faculty, not first generation to college, and he had been better prepared with information about what to request and undertake as a junior scholar. Consequently he was offered and received summer support before the beginning of his contract, while Maricela did not know that this was possible and so struggled with finances at the beginning of the year and before receipt of her first paycheck in October. The faculty position was also her first experience with the cultural incongruity of academe. As a Latina, she enacted and operated under taken-for-granted and culturally grounded collectivist expectations that those around her would be welcoming and looking out for her as a new member of the community in the same way that her family and community would look out for her at home. What she learned instead is academe's expectation that its members speak for and take care of themselves (Oliva et al., 2013). She did not immediately understand but learned that if she expressed a need, something might be done to address it. Until then, she might have to suffer in silence given that others were not monitoring how she was doing.

This lack of attention to her needs repeatedly stung in that it seemed to reflect a lack of caring from colleagues. White and senior colleagues' inattention, aloofness, and occasional hostility was a very different experience from the communitarian orientation of Latino and female culture, even that of the state agency in which Maricela had been treated as an important part of a larger whole. Her upbringing in community to that point reflected a "*somos*/we are" rather than a "*soy*/I am" collectivist worldview (Museus and Jayakumar, 2012).

Despite now working in a border institution, Maricela quickly learned about navigating academe alone and having to take care of and fend for herself. Indeed, her experience at the state agency and in doctoral study had initially been similar. Returning to a culturally congruent border community had lulled her into the false sense that she was "home" again. While the community outside the university looked and seemed like home, the institution itself and the culture inside of it turned out not to be. The institution in the community was not truly of the community because there was a cultural incongruity between those in it and those outside.

The forms of neglect, cultural incongruity, and microaggressions (Sue et al., 2007) that Maricela experienced as a new faculty member were multifaceted. These included:

- grudging acceptance, primarily because institutional leaders expressed it, that Latina/os had things to offer the institution and its future.
- superficial understanding of the diversity of thought that Latinx scholars represented in/for the department. While acknowledging her different gender and color, senior scholars were often surprised and unhappy that Maricela's expressed views differed from theirs.

- little access to decision-making influence and authority, given her junior rank and the view of K-12 senior scholars that she lacked knowledge about the field. On the other hand, the white male junior scholar participated socially and was embraced as one of the boys by senior male scholars and had more of a hand in shaping departmental decisions.
- persistently negative and disempowering feedback that undermined her confidence and sense of readiness to participate in the professoriate. Maricela experienced "imposter syndrome" (Laux, 2018) and a sense that she did not belong. When she realized this was happening, Maricela engaged in affirming self-talk, reminding herself that as an Ivy League and UT Austin graduate, she had a lot to offer.[5]

As illustrated by the description of Maricela's *antecedent* experience at the state higher education agency, she had come to the institution with significant information and knowledge about higher education in Texas and developments that UTEP was undertaking in response to litigation. Having just spent the previous seven years at the state agency, she had more insider cultural and professional knowledge than white faculty in the department from origins outside of the state. However, in the hierarchical and gendered structure of the department, that did not translate into professional or cultural legitimacy as a faculty member, scholar, woman, or person.

Incorporation

Maricela would move several times before finding an institution where her ideas and research objectives in higher education found fertile ground. The first institution after UTEP was another border university to which she was recruited for her administrative knowledge to direct a cooperative doctoral program with UT Austin. Once there, she found and had to navigate hidden minefields, including a sexual misconduct scandal involving a program full professor; enmity between the dean and provost that positioned her in the crosshairs between them while trying to move the program forward; a departmental faculty unfamiliar with, reluctant to, or still learning how to step up to the research and service demands of doctoral instruction; and a generally toxic environment in which senior faculty members were not averse to fabricating complaints as leverage over those they wanted to keep in line. Still untenured, she left the institution after two years for a full-fledged program in higher education at Texas A&M. It seemed the perfect new place to be, but when she arrived at the new job, the program was very different from when she interviewed.

One senior program faculty member of color had departed over the summer for a position as department chair on the East Coast. The two remaining senior full professors in the program area were in open conflict about her departure and often not speaking—one saying the other had not advocated enough to try to retain her. The department as a whole was considered top-heavy with senior white scholars who were reportedly not staying current in their scholarship or reflecting current thinking. In that context, junior scholars were nevertheless given wide latitude to work on their research, and Maricela was able to do so, given no administrative assignments.

After a year and a half within the program for higher education, upper administrators decided to make additional changes by bringing in a new department chair. The person brought in was evidently tasked with changing the personnel and culture of the department. In the first year, beloved senior faculty members in some program areas were "retired" or demoted, and sacred cows of tradition or practice were unceremoniously set aside. While Maricela had supported hiring the new department chair, she also was troubled by unilateral decision-making around personnel that tended to undermine departmental community. Given her support for the chair as a member of the search committee, his actions drew negative attention to her and eroded senior faculty members' support. Her own discomfort with the chair's interpersonal interactions within the department, coupled with a growing awareness of the larger institution's resistance to diversity concerns, convinced her that she should not remain. She looked again at opportunities elsewhere.

Her current institution, UTSA, has indeed been the best place to work, both for the city and institutional and departmental environments. The university's designation as a HSI with a mission to serve the predominately Latinx regional community has meant that she has not had to justify or rationalize her research interests or agenda. Because UTSA is also aspiring to becoming a tier-one university, the institution has also promoted both inclusion and research excellence. Despite internal politics about the likelihood of actually achieving both of those goals, the institution has until now held fast to the idea of moving concurrently toward both goals. Maricela has herself been key to the development of the institution's master's program in higher education and a higher education emphasis to the existing doctoral program. In the process, she grew the higher education faculty from one (herself) to seven or more specialized higher education faculty members of different ranks.

Despite a health crisis that year, Maricela was successful in her tenure bid. Several years later, she was recruited to administrative positions outside of the institution. Although a finalist for department chair, the hiring institution chose not instead to fill the position temporarily on an interim basis. Maricela's interest in administration prompted a job offer at UTSA as associate vice provost for academic and faculty support, where she served on a half-time basis for three and a half years. She is now Associate Dean of the College of Education and Human Development with similar responsibilities for faculty issues and development.

After the successful tenure application and her decades of academic and administrative experience, it can be said that Maricela has achieved the level of incorporation at her institution to which all faculty aspire. She has responsibilities regarding training for new faculty hires and the development of institutional faculty for long-term success. She monitors the institution's departmental mentoring programs and was tapped to mentor a Latina assistant professor. Given her own experiences with needing mentoring and the lack of senior Latinas in the junior faculty member's department, in 2016 Maricela agreed to serve as a mentor to co-author Nevarez.

The Mentoring Relationship

The mentoring commenced after Lucinda's third-year review at the recommendation of the department's faculty review committee to the department chair. The department chair, an African American male scholar, concurred with their desire to support Lucinda's long-term success and believed that culturally sensitive mentoring would help identify and respond to her needs. Since engaging in mentoring, the two have refocused efforts on Lucinda's publishing, identified strategies to move collaborative projects from in-progress to submission, made use of existing policies to create opportunities for success, and have strategized about how best to navigate tensions within the department.

As an institution, UTSA has organized mentoring support for new faculty members, which is significantly different from Maricela's experience. Furthermore Lucinda's department is populated with more women and faculty of color, a fact that seems to have resulted in recognizing the value of a collectivist approach to supporting their new faculty member. This has included understanding that cultural congruity was needed in the mentoring relationship and taking time to go outside of the department to find a willing mentor. Coming to the mentoring relationship with extensive multi-site experience and an awareness of challenges around what it means to be an assistant professor, Maricela strives to be a mentor to Nevarez that she wishes she could have had.

Lucinda's Story: Evolving Authenticity and Mentoring to Bridge the Gap

Evolving Authenticity

A key factor in the success of faculty, particularly those of color, is the accessibility of knowledge related to the tenure process and addressing the unique early challenges that these faculty face (Thompson, 2018).

Prior to her faculty position, while she was still a postdoctoral scholar, Lucinda was surrounded by emerging researchers addressing issues of health equity in new and exciting ways. While her postdoctoral experience exposed her to the rigors of research, it was not as informative about tenure. The tenure process itself is often unclear, and tenure expectations vary between disciplines and institutions. Added to this variability, the lack of exposure presented a challenge for Lucinda's ability to adapt to the environment. Being the first in her family to graduate college and receive postgraduate degrees, she lacked any network that could provide insight about how to navigate the academic setting and acquire tenure. She entered academe unable to contextualize the experience and lacking an accessible source of knowledge about how to navigate the tenure process. Moreover, there were no readily available materials or individuals that could frame the tenure process and academic setting in a way that was culturally translatable. Like many Latina faculty, she came into academia with a culturally based perspective that prioritized community and collaboration (Ek, Cerecer, Alanis, and Rodriguez, 2010), a stark contrast to the independent focus often expected during the tenure process. Early in her academic career, her professional network encompassed individuals like her who were entering academia and learning to navigate the system themselves. While this created some support for her as an emerging scholar, it did little to enhance her understanding of how to successfully manage tenure.

One surprising aspect of academic life was the role that cultivating relationships played within the department and tenure process. Although previous mentors and allies had told her about the presence of social and political elements in academic settings, she was not prepared for how persistent they were. Lucinda came into academia under the assumption that there would be an employee/employer dynamic. While she was prepared to undertake projects and move them forward, she felt uncertain about her role and ability to lead in certain areas. She was encouraged to take leadership roles, yet when she moved forward, her efforts were met with resistance. She was often told that there was a role that the wider department needed to play in approving changes and that things did not depend on her decisions alone.

A key area where this became a factor was when she experienced a significant illness her first year in the academy. While this illness presented a formidable obstacle in her ability to perform basic day-to-day tasks, she continued to forge through, unaware that there were mechanisms through the university that would have provided her some reprieve from work-related responsibilities and challenges. In the context of this serious illness, Lucinda finished her year disappointed in her productivity. Her lack of familiarity with the system and process meant that she was not aware that she could request to halt her tenure clock to address her health issues. Instead she pushed through, placing her health at further risk and limiting how productive she appeared in her annual review. It was not until learning of another colleague's petition for consideration for medical conditions and after a conversation with an administrator who wondered why she had not asked for similar relief that she became aware that doing so was an option.

This highlights the importance that knowledge about the tenure process and institutional policies can have in navigating that system. Had she known, she would have petitioned for time to focus on health, and then her productivity would also not have seemed so poor. Within the often-ambiguous probationary system, it is hard for new faculty to know what they do not know. Such was the case for Lucinda and her illness. At times, things are straightforward, but most of the time there is some lack of clarity. Questions like "How many publications do we need?" and "What service opportunities are representative of our commitment to the university and department?" abound.

A challenge for her in addressing this lack of knowledge was that Lucinda was experiencing academic life much like other Latinas, in isolation (Urrieta, Méndez, and Rodríguez, 2014; Thompson, 2018). At times this isolation was system created; at other times it was self-imposed isolation. Lucinda rarely encountered people who reflected her culture or life experience that were working in the same capacity. Not only did she experience difference in terms of ethnocultural identity, but also in life-stage transitions. She was older than many fellow postdoctoral and faculty colleagues, had been married, and was a single parent. These combined attributes exacerbated the knowledge gap, as there was no one that she knew who shared the faculty and life stage experience and could help explore successful ways of navigating it.

Important social connections were lost to her, given that many of the faculty social interactions involved happy hours or dinners, many of which she was unable to attend because of her single-parent status. Yet such interactions are key to the department in that they not only foster community and collegiality, they provide opportunities to establish and tap into networks of knowledge about the system and foster perceptions about her that could potentially influence senior faculty during her tenure review.

Faced with this lack in available knowledge and resources to draw knowledge from, Lucinda often traversed the tenure journey on her own, learning by trial and error about the academic landscape. A consequence of applying this trial-and-error approach meant she was finding out information later than she needed it (like the option around her illness). It also meant she was learning primarily via reprimands or corrective actions to remedy her "inaccurate" approaches. Repeatedly hearing "no" and "not like that" created even more isolation and contributed to her questioning her abilities.

In preparation for her third-year review, she struggled to find what a tenure packet looked like and sought to gain a general understanding from internet sites and conversations she overheard. For example, her third-year packet was submitted containing a writing-style formatting error because the required style was not highlighted. In her review meeting, she was told that knowledge of the required use of that style was assumed. The senior faculty stated in their review that the inclusion of this error suggested she had not given sufficient attention to her packet.

While the communal aspects of learning and working together strongly appeal to Lucinda, they are not the predominant style in academia, which focuses on more individualized endeavors (Tuitt, Hanna, Martinez, Salazar, and Griffin, 2009). Lucinda's approach to entering the academic setting was a communal approach, so it was jarring to have to work in isolation and independently a majority of the time.

In many of these instances, it seemed to Lucinda that the academy and those in it were speaking a different language than she was. On both sides, this language permeated expectations, interactions, and experiences. Lucinda was operating at home from a language that emphasized elements of community and family, while the academic environment was communicating in a language steeped in rugged individualism and independence. This ongoing language barrier contributed to her assumption that if resources and information were available, they would be presented and offered, while institutionally it was apparently anticipated that if she needed those resources and information, she would request them. Because she did not immediately recognize the communal versus individual difference in approach, she did not know to ask for resources and information, resulting in going without them and instead trying to figure things out for herself.

The question that kept coming up for her was "Where did they hear about that?" or "How did they know that?" It was surprising how many of her colleagues replied that they just knew or had networks familiar with tenure and academia to guide them toward what resources to seek out and request. In contrast, she was not advised of things she could do even after mentioning her illness, so she assumed that there was nothing that could be done for someone in her situation. In reality, the assumption within academe seemed to be that if she needed time off or a break, she would ask for it. But how can you ask for something that you do not know is a possibility? In this context, Lucinda's cultural orientation as Latina in a department with predominately non-Latino colleagues led to miscommunication and a lack of support during a life-threatening illness requiring hospitalization, which could have led to her death.

Lucinda found herself reluctant to explicitly ask for help in part so as not to appear uninformed to her colleagues. This may be related to imposter syndrome (Laux, 2018) and from being a first-generation academic unsure of her place and ability in the academic setting. The messages she repeatedly received indicated that a lot of things were common knowledge. That for her it was not common knowledge reinforced the idea of not belonging and possibly lacking the capabilities and knowledge she should have had. In a sense, this knowledge and language differential created and reinforced otherness for Lucinda in academia (Good, Rattan, and Dweck, 2012; Laux, 2018).

The lack of knowledge to draw from and an inability to access networks and resources that foster knowledge about the system fed and reinforced Lucinda's insecurities related to her academic role and fitness for academia. She wondered if she were worthy and capable as a faculty member. In a negative spiral, this lack of confidence exacerbated her hesitation to request information and support services, fearing it would validate others' assumptions about her inadequacies. She tried not to ask about things and to instead figure things out herself.

Additionally the lack of others who shared her identity, ethnocultural background, and life stage as a mother raising young children reinforced a sense that he did not belong. In essence, for Lucinda, the lack of representation of other Latina faculty implied academia was a setting in which Latinas did not belong. This reinforced her isolation, creating a belief that she should not risk being identified as lacking intellect by asking about elements of academia or the tenure process that others seemed to know about and had well in hand.

Lucinda's sense was that nonminority colleagues seemed to be able to successfully manage the demands of academia while she perceived it as a constant struggle. She did not consider the role that academic support networks could play in aiding her colleagues through the tenure process (Gutiérrez y Muhs, Niemann, González, and Harris, 2012). Furthermore it was disheartening to find herself unable to identify similar academic support networks that could give her that same guidance. Additionally, while departmental peers were bonding and supporting each other through tenure, she was felt as though she was going through the tenure process alone.

Lucinda approached her third-year review lacking familiarity with the process, leaving her to rely heavily on university policies and internet searches to understand what a tenure package should consist of and how materials should appear. Subsequently in her third-year review, the review committee indicated that she could have gone further in highlighting particular areas of her work and that areas of her packet needed to be visually better represented. Following that review, Lucinda encountered other junior faculty who referenced how valuable it was to have had others review their third-year review packets prior to submission. Those faculty (none of whom were persons of color) had family members or previous mentors who were tenured faculty at other academic institutions offer pre-submission assistance. Since she did not, Lucinda's packet lacked some of the nuances that others were able to include and so compared poorly.

In addition to these systemic challenges of traversing the tenure process, there have also been critical culturally based dynamics that impact more directly the relationships and work that Latinas do in the academic setting. Faculty of color report having to do more service, isolation, differences in evaluative weight given to research areas, and being challenged more by students in the classroom setting (Thompson, 2018). Lucinda experienced some of that targeting by students, faculty, and administrators primarily due to her identification as a Latina within the academic setting. In her teaching, especially early on, students challenged her in more personal ways than they did her white male counterparts.

Once when she was trying to administer a quiz, students simply ignored her and tried to initiate a classroom vote to decide if they would take the quiz or not. In another instance, this differential treatment was also experienced in many of her interactions with faculty and staff from varying institutions. The result was that it was challenging for Lucinda to feel anything but "other" in her first year of academia. Although part of a larger group of new faculty, she was frequently ignored or excluded as a member of that group at faculty and committee meetings. During one faculty meeting, a thirty-minute faculty discussion was even held about whether her vote on a matter should count due to a technicality with her appointment. On other occasions, she offered opinions or insights and had them ignored or diminished, only to hear them later applauded when repeated by white faculty members. In one instance, a white female colleague on a committee shared her excitement that Lucinda was added to the committee because "now the committee has a Hispanic." This colleague did not convey appreciation for any of the skills or talents that Lucinda might bring to that committee, but only her reassurance that the committee would now be counted as diverse.

Mentoring to Bridge the Gap

In her graduate studies, Lucinda had been the fortunate recipient of advising and mentorship via a loose network of fluid and unstructured mentoring. The primary mentoring relationship that she had as a graduate student reflected the top-down, one-to-one mentoring style often associated with hierarchical advising relationships. Lucinda was comfortable in her student role, but as she transitioned from student to postdoctoral scholar, her participation as a Kellogg Health Scholar Fellow provided an extensive model for mentoring that required fellows to identify multiple mentors. Lucinda struggled to identify scholars in her discipline area that could serve in this capacity. Although the program stressed the role of mentors that she did not already know, she did not get help with how to successfully identify and implement those mentoring relationships.

In the postdoctoral setting, Lucinda found herself working from a hierarchical student-based framework in which she depended on a senior faculty member for direction, yet this approach was not proving itself as effective. While she approached the mentoring relationships expecting direction from the mentors, the identified mentors were waiting for Lucinda to guide the direction of the relationship. Additionally she mostly chose mentors who were remote to her institution, nearing retirement, or leading research institutes that were so demanding they were not able to contribute thoughtfully to her needs. Lucinda also found herself unsure of and uncomfortable with engaging the mentoring relationship. The lack of guidance and her limited familiarity with how to direct these mentoring relationships left her unsure and consequently unwilling to make the time to access them.

Indeed Lucinda approached mentoring from a perspective that assumed the relationship would be nurturing, supportive, directive, and interpersonal. What she experienced instead were mentoring relationships that were authoritative, distant, superficial, and one-directional. In most instances she heard little to no feedback from these types of mentors, except to have her work on their specific projects. On many occasions, feedback was limited to addressing missteps or correcting project-related issues. This created an atmosphere in the mentoring relationship that prevented accessing the mentor for guidance and infused the postdoctoral mentoring relationship with fear and anxiety. She was not able to capitalize on these relationships, and they came to reflect the disconnect between her expectation of mentoring and what she actually received.

There were nonetheless elements in mentoring relationships that Lucinda saw as a positive influence in her evolution toward authenticity in the academy. Those mentoring relationships that recognized and acknowledged the ethnocultural influences in her work and life were among the most successful experiences. In addition, those mentoring relationships that created a safe space and incorporated diversity in perspectives and disciplinary focus became the mentoring relationships that are still most impactful. Mentors who shared a similar cultural background or those who may have a differing background but were open to hers and acknowledged the importance of cultural elements like family, community, and collaboration became the mentors with whom she was able to establish long-standing positive mentoring relationships. Most of these mentors took time to get to know her in a personal way, and this helped to establish a critical relational part of the mentoring experience.

Successful mentors accounted for factors that she identified as key to her work-life balance and helped connect issues relevant to her life with meaningful research initiatives. Because these mentors understood the communal aspect of Lucinda's perspective, they were appropriately supportive and encouraging when familial or social dynamics posed potential distractions to her trajectory. As these mentors established a foundational relationship with Lucinda, they were able to create an environment that felt safe. This allowed her to feel comfortable asking her mentor for resources, knowledge, and access to networks. These relationships also cultivated a space where she could talk in confidence about those areas of academia with which she needed help. These relationships also pushed her to recognize and appreciate the social and cultural capital that she brings to the academic setting.

It can be an unanticipated challenge to have senior faculty characterize a desire for mentoring as a weakness. For example, an early discussion of Lucinda's desire for mentoring was described as her not having evolved enough to have outgrown the need for a mentor. In contrast, she thought of her mentoring as long-term relationships that would grow and evolve as she did. Such a view of mentoring relationship reflected a cultural perspective that included the presumption that her mentor would become a part of her larger social system and that the relationship itself would continue indefinitely. To be described in the third-year review as not having grown out of the need for mentoring in contrast to two white faculty members who were described as having done so implied a deficiency on her part for not having done the same.

Following the third-year review, Lucinda's department recommended connecting her with a mentor to offer support and insight on the academic environment and tenure process. In recognition of Lucinda's expressed desire to have a mentor that reflected her diverse background, she was connected with Maricela. Lucinda and her department were hopeful that through this mentoring relationship, Lucinda could establish a support system that was sensitive to her Latina experience in higher education.

A key positive indicator for Lucinda immediately upon engaging with Maricela was her expressed recognition of the importance of mentorship for faculty, particularly for faculty of color. This shared insight helped Lucinda set aside the negative messages she had been receiving about her perceived weakness for desiring mentoring. In much of their first meeting, Maricela and Lucinda engaged in small talk, getting to know one another, which was important to establishing relational dynamics that become critical to later stages of mentoring. Because of the time spent familiarizing themselves with each other, Lucinda was able to develop trust and comfort with sharing elements of the academic setting and tenure that were confounding her.

In recognition of the importance that Lucinda ascribes to her familial relationships, she and Maricela have connected at familial events in the community. These gatherings have given Lucinda the chance to tap into that mentoring experience in a new way. Through these interactions, she is able to socially connect with her mentor, who is able to get a better understanding of who she is and what she values. Once the two had established some comfort with each other, they created plans that included necessary and achievable tenure goals for Lucinda.

This interaction highlights the importance for Latinas of balancing the relational and directive aspect of the mentoring relationship. Maricela took the time to learn about Lucinda as a person but was also able to give invaluable insight about necessary tasks to navigate the academic setting and tenure. Lucinda and Maricela have spoken numerous times about mentorship, each sharing previous experiences to develop a shared understanding of expectations and what mentorship represents.

A key benefit of the current mentoring relationship for Lucinda has been the opportunity to feel less isolated and more a part of the academic experience. When in previous instances she has thought that she was the only one experiencing a dilemma or issue, the feeling was accompanied by a sense of inadequacy. Through the mentoring relationship, Lucinda is able to share her experiences and learn that, in fact, they arise for many faculty of color. She no longer sees them as personal deficits but as systemic barriers that, because of her identity, she may be more at risk of experiencing. Just as important, she is also able to draw from Maricela's extensive knowledge of institutional practices to navigate the complex academic setting.

Discussion

Voice

Reading across the experience of the two Latina faculty members from different generations, it is clear that finding or developing voice in academe has been an issue for both. Even after Latinas find their voice—as in Maricela's case with the state higher education agency—the hierarchical, predominately white, and male-oriented departments worked to diminish her confidence and outspokenness. In the entry phase, she worked to hold on to her voice and sense of self despite persistent messages that in higher education she was an outsider and other (i.e., junior, not K-12, not male, not white). She fought to resist negative messaging with self-affirming strategies that reminded her of past accomplishments and her ability to shape and transform higher education.

For Lucinda, finding voice and confidence continues to be an issue. Her input on challenging topics, such as those related to diversity, is too often negated or disputed. Interactions with faculty colleagues signal that she is not truly valued and have made her feel that speaking up is unwelcome and dangerous. Before being paired with a mentor, her reaction had been to internalize her views and to make her way through the academic journey alone. However, when she did not know to ask for specific support and resources during her illness, she felt blamed for not having been more insistent in asking for help. Thus, the message she received was that both using her voice and not using her voice resulted in negative consequences. What is emerging for Lucinda now is a desire and need to use her voice more skillfully and effectively. She was asked recently to join a committee for her discipline's national organization, where she plans to hone her skills and confidence as she provides her views on policies related to national standards for her discipline's approach to diversity.

Socialization

One of the peculiarities of Texas institutions is that higher education programs are infrequent, small, and usually housed in departments with much larger K-12 programs. The departments in the South Texas border where Maricela applied to work did not already have higher education offerings. She was the first or only higher-education faculty member or the only Latina. Senior faculty members did not know a lot about the discipline and how its values and organizing assumptions are not the same as for K-12 programs. Compared to her experiences in government, socialization as a faculty member was disempowering. In government, Maricela had been prodded to speak and operate from a position of authenticity, whereas colleagues in academe encouraged her assimilation into their way of thinking and rarely accommodated her ethnic and gender difference. Maricela came to explicitly recognize and work against disempowering language and behaviors of colleagues during the entry stage of navigating academe.

For Lucinda, early professional socialization without Latina colleagues was isolating and reinforced internal doubts about her ability to succeed as a faculty member. The lack of colleagues that looked like her or came from her Latina background implied that individuals like her do not belong in a faculty position or do not remain. A sense of isolation was deepened when she was often overlooked and ignored during faculty meeting discussions about the needs and accomplishments of junior faculty. These experiences created for her an atmosphere of uncertainty and fear within the university that she is now working to overcome. While experiencing the university as a dangerous place, Lucinda at the same time has an overwhelming need to successfully overcome the environment to prove to herself and others that Latinas do not just belong in academic settings, but they enhance them.

Mentoring

In Maricela's case, formal mentoring programs were not in place at her institutions, and she had no senior disciplinary mentors to work with her. She either did not receive mentoring, what was offered was incongruent with her identity and values as a policy-informed Latina, or mentoring was not culturally competent and totally disregarded her identity as Latina. Her career included several moves among institutions to find the right supportive environment. Eventually she advanced in leadership and administrative ranks to a position in the provost's office.

Lucinda contends that one of the greatest gains in the past two years has been the insightful and consistent support that she has received through Maricela's mentoring. The two have met to discuss issues ranging from tenure expectations, the university environment, and advice on how to navigate complex interpersonal interaction that can arise in the academic setting. Their mentoring relationship is more reflective of what Lucinda anticipated, and she expects that it will be continue to be productive and supportive. Their shared background has further created for Lucinda a sense that Maricela understands her competing demands as daughter, mother, community member, and faculty colleague that she must consider when making career and project decisions. By helping to unpack some of what happens in the academic context, Maricela has helped Lucinda navigate it and has alleviated some of the anxiety and uncertainty tied to tenure. Key efforts have included Lucinda working with Maricela to develop a more streamlined strategy to accomplish tenure-related goals.

Conclusion

While Latinas remain underrepresented among the faculty, institutions are increasingly better prepared to facilitate their success through mentoring. The experience of these two Latina scholars from different generations has much to offer in helping us understand past and current environments for Latinas in academe. Institutions are now more aware than when Maricela started her career about the need to offer opportunities for Latinas to achieve success in ways that are culturally and gender authentic. New formal mentoring programs for faculty in which Maricela and Lucinda now participate help faculty to navigate their entry and incorporation into the professoriate. Unfortunately what has not changed is the need to improve cultural competence within colleges and universities so awareness of the issues translates into actual skill at managing and incorporating diversity. As Lucinda's story illustrates, Latinas continue to experience academe as isolating and culturally disempowering, if not hostile. While progress is being made, it is excruciatingly slow in occurring. Accelerating the rate of improvement for Latinas is more likely through renewed and intensified efforts to recruit Latinx faculty, particularly Latinas, so there is a critical mass within programs and departments. We will see institutions make progress when the proportion of Latina faculty more closely reflects the diversity in the increasingly Latinx and increasingly female population of admitted and enrolled college students.

Notes

1 ASHE is the acronym for the Association for the Study of Higher Education, the discipline's research association.

2 The terms *antecedent, entry,* and *incorporation* are the author's own to discuss phases of the journey into faculty life.
3 The litigation began before the federal term HSI was created and came into wide use. However, plaintiffs argued that underfunding was improperly associated with the student demographics (predominately Latinx students) of border universities.
4 Adams case litigation refers to a series of lawsuits brought against the U.S. federal government to force compliance with desegregation as required by the Civil Rights Act of 1964. From 1970 until 1990, various plaintiffs sued the Department of Education to force them to stop de facto segregation in higher education. For more, see www.clearinghouse.net/detail.php?id=11091.
5 Maricela recognized the negative psychological effect of the negativity constantly directed her way. To help affirm herself in the face of that, she ordered her undergraduate college graduation ring from Yale. As a low-income student, she had considered the ring a luxury. However, as a first-year faculty member, she used it to buoy her confidence and to resist repeated microaggressions.

References

Acevedo-Gil, N., and Madrigal-Garcia, Y. (2018). Mentoring among Latina/o scholars: Enacting spiritual activism to navigate academia. *American Journal of Education, 124*(3), 313–344.

Chesney-Lind, M., Okamoto, S., and Irwin, K. (2006). Thoughts on feminist mentoring: Experiences of faculty members from two generations in the academy. *Critical Criminology, 14*(1), 1–21.

Christie, H. (2014). Peer mentoring in higher education: Issues of power and control. *Teaching Higher Education, 19*(8), 955–965.

Delgado Bernal, D. D., and Villalpando, O. (2002). An apartheid of knowledge in academia: The struggle over the "Legitimate" knowledge of faculty of color. *Equity & Excellence in Education, 35*(2), 169–180.

Ek, L. D., Cerecer, P. D. Q., Alanis, I., and Rodriguez, M. A. (2010). "I don't belong here": Chicanas/Latinas at a Hispanic serving institution creating community through Muxerista mentoring. *Equity & Excellence in Education, 43*(4), 539–553.

Faurer, J., Sutton, C., and Worster, L. (2014). Faculty mentoring: Shaping a program. *Contemporary Issues in Education Research, 7*(2), 151.

Gibson, S. K. (2006). Mentoring of women faculty: The role of organizational politics and culture. *Innovative Higher Education, 31*(1), 63–79.

Gonzales, L. D., Murakami, E., and Núñez, A-M. (2013). Latina faculty in the labyrinth: Constructing and contesting legitimacy in Hispanic serving institutions. *Journal of Educational Foundations, 27,* 65–89.

Good, C., Rattan, A., and Dweck, C. S. (2012). Why do women opt out? Sense of belonging and women's representation in mathematics. *Journal of Personality and Social Psychology, 102*(4), 700–717.

Gutiérrez y Muhs, G., Niemann, Y. F., González, C. G., and Harris, A. P. (2012). *Presumed incompetent: The intersections of race and class for women in academia.* Logan, UT: Utah State University Press.

Johnson, W. B. (2007). *On being a mentor: A guide for higher education faculty.* Mahwah, NJ: Lawrence Erlbaum Associates.

Laux, S. E. (2018). *Experiencing the imposter syndrome in academia: Women faculty members' perception of the tenure and promotion process* (Order No. 10822836). ProQuest Dissertations & Theses Global. (2070929379). Retrieved from https://login.libweb.lib.utsa.edu/login?url=https://search.proquest.com/docview/2070929379?accountid=7122

Mkandawire-Valhmu, L., Kako, P. M., and Stevens, P. E. (2010). Mentoring women faculty of color in nursing academia: Creating an environment that supports scholarly growth and retention. *Nursing Outlook, 58*(3), 135–141.

Museus, S. D., and Jayakumar, U. M. (2012). *Creating campus cultures: Fostering success among racially diverse student populations*. New York, NY: Routledge.

Oliva, M., Rodriguez, M., Alanis, I., and Quijada, P. (2013). At home in the academy: Latina faculty counterstories and resistances. *Journal of Educational Foundations, 27*(1–2), 91–109.

Ortegon, R. R. (2013). *LULAC v. Richards: The class action lawsuit that prompted the south Texas border initiative and enhanced access to higher education for Mexican Americans living along the south Texas border* (Doctoral Dissertation). Retrieved from https://reository.library.northeastern.edu/files/neu:1117

Sue, D. W., Capodilupo, C. M., Torino, G. C., Bucceri, J. M., Holder, A. M., Nadal, K. L., and Esquilin, M. (2007). Racial microaggressions in everyday life: Implications for clinical practice. *American Psychologist, 62*(4), 271–286.

Thompson, C. Q. (2018). Recruitment, retention, and mentoring faculty of color: The chronicle continues. *New Directions for Higher Education, 2018*(143), 47–54.

Tuitt, F., Hanna, M., Martinez, L. M., Salazar, M. C., and Griffin, R. (2009). Teaching in the line of fire: Faculty of color in the academy. *Thought & Action, 25*, 65–74.

Turner, C. S. V., and Gonzales, J. C. (2014). *Modeling mentoring across race/ethnicity and gender: Practices to cultivate the next generation of diverse faculty*. Sterling, VA: Stylus Publishing, LLC.

Urrieta, L., Méndez, L., and Rodríguez, E. (2014). "A moving target": A critical race analysis of Latina/o faculty experiences, perspectives, and reflections on the tenure and promotion process. *International Journal of Qualitative Studies in Education, 28*(10), 1149–1168.

Watson, E. D., Mack, D., and Camacho, M. M. (2012). *Mentoring faculty of color: Essays on professional development and advancement in colleges and universities*. Jefferson, NC: McFarland & Company, Inc., Publishers.

Zambrana, R. E., Ray, R., Espino, M. M., Castro, C., Cohen, B. D., and Eliason, J. (2015). "Don't leave us behind": The importance of mentoring for underrepresented minority faculty. *American Educational Research Journal, 52*(1), 40–72.

3 "In Academia, But Not of It"[1]—Redefining What It Means to Serve

Judy Marquez Kiyama and Leslie Gonzales

In the seminal book, *Presumed Incompetent: The Intersections of Race and Class for Women in Academia,* Holling et al. (2012) wrote, "The way we have chosen to walk in the academy is a new path, one that few of our ancestors have traveled, so none of the womyn in our families know how to show us the way" (p. 251). And at the end of the chapter, the authors concluded, "We are three womyn of color in academia, but not of it" (p. 265).

As two Latina, first-generation college students and recently tenured women of color, Holling, Fu, and Barber's writing resonates with us. Like most associate professors and especially women of color associate professors, we have found ourselves barraged with a range of new service opportunities and requests (O'Meara, Kuvaeva, Nyunt, Waugaman, and Jackson, 2017). The requests are often framed in discourses that suggest that, as tenured faculty, we are now fuller participants in a community of scholars and in a position to serve our institution in more substantial ways.

However, like Holling, Fu, and Barber, we believe *that we are only in, but not of* our institutions. Thus, although we are expected to serve in more labor-intensive ways, in ways that ostensibly signify a deeper commitment to our institution—and often in connection with devalued or undervalued service roles (Broido, Brown, Stygles, and Bronkema, 2015)—we find ourselves guided by radically different purposes. And based on literature that elevates the voice of Latinas and women of color, more broadly, we know we are not alone (Baez, 2000; Delgado-Bernal, 2007; Gutiérrez y Muhs, Flores Niemann, González, and Harris, 2012). In short, it is not our institutional commitment that drives our service, but the commitment we have to our communities and to advance justice in any way we can.

Therefore, the goal of this chapter is to share our dispositions toward and engagement in service as two post-tenure Latinas who are actively and strategically resisting taken-for-granted frameworks and notions of service. Drawing from Chicana feminist epistemology (CFE) (Calderón, Delgado Bernal, Pérez Huber, Malagón, and Vélez, 2012; Delgado

Bernal, 1998; Elenes and Delgado Bernal, 2010), we discuss how our locations in a white, racist, and patriarchal society has armed us with intuition and knowledge that compel us to critique and deconstruct normative notions of service in order to serve in ways that align with our epistemological and historical foundations. Below, we provide a brief discussion of CFE before describing how each of us is approaching service in our post-tenure careers.

Chicana Feminist Epistemology (CFE)

Epistemology can be understood as a way of knowing, or a knowledge system. It is how people evaluate, valuate, organize, and make sense of the world. In a world where policy-making and institution-building are underwritten by whiteness, capitalistic, patriarchal, and Western scientistic interests, it can be difficult to elevate ways of knowing that challenge such values and habits. This is why Delgado Bernal (1998) reminds us that questions of epistemology are always enwrapped in "power, ethics, politics, and survival" (p. 556). In this chapter, we draw on Delgado-Bernal's work on CFE to critique how service has historically been conceptualized in academia and to articulate our dispositions toward and engagement in service as two post-tenure Latinas.

As a framework, CFE provides language and tools that allow women of color, but particularly Chicanas, to challenge dominant knowledge systems. CFE was conceptualized as a response to the ways in which mainstream education has failed Chicanas and, more specifically, as a "means to resist epistemological racism" (Delgado Bernal, 1998, p. 556). For example, CFE points out how, in the context of the U.S., valuable knowledge is defined by the principles of scientism, which elevates objectivity and detachment and dismisses experience as a source of knowledge. CFE upends the normalcy of this knowledge system and asserts that knowledge begins with our own realities (Elenes and Delgado Bernal, 2010) and is grounded in historical and cultural experiences and often in collective memory. In this way, CFE elevates Chicanas as knowers and asserts that our/their knowledge is not only legitimate but valuable.

As noted above, typically epistemology is discussed in the context of research and methodological debates (Delgado Bernal, 1998; Gonzales, 2018). However, CFE is more than methods. It is a distinctive disposition—a way of moving about and surviving in a society not made for women of color. For example, Delgado Bernal (1998) uses CFE to theorize how her scholarship, service, and personal life as a mother are intimately and necessarily connected. In the same way, CFE helps us problematize service, which is often framed as a way that faculty can give back to their institutions or academic disciplines (Ward, 2003) to offer an alternative conceptualization. Below, we show how our location and experiences as low-income or working-class women of color, first-generation college students have compelled us to center experiences and insights gifted to us by our families while growing up on our respective ranches where community needs surpassed any one individual's interests.

Cultural Histories, Intuitions, and Knowledges

Judy

I had just turned in what I thought was the final draft of my dissertation to my advisor. As the feeling of relief swept over me, my advisor emailed back and said he wanted to hear more of my voice in the dissertation. I struggled with figuring out what that might mean. I had been presented with a dissertation task that fell outside of the Western knowledge system's demands for objectivity and positivism—the rules I was trained to follow. He nudged me with a reminder of the framework I was using, that of funds of knowledge. Funds of knowledge "refer to the historically accumulated and culturally developed bodies of knowledge and skills essential for household or individual functioning and well-being" (Moll, Amanti, Neff, and Gonzalez, 1992, p. 133). These cultural forms of knowledge serve as a powerful foundation from which to build curriculum that honors the history and bodies of knowledge of immigrant, working-class, and often first-generation Latina/o families.

My own family experiences have helped me to recognize and honor the various forms of knowledge of the communities with whom I work—most often communities of color from working-class, immigrant, and refugee backgrounds—and my advisor had urged me to share about this. After struggling with the recognition that I would have to be vulnerable in my dissertation, I shared the following in chapter one, titled "Representation of Voice":

> If my life were a play or a novel, my experiences would have foreshadowed the type of research [and now I can expand this to service and teaching] that I do. I am a first-generation, Mexican-American college student. Neither of my parents graduated from a four-year institution and both held working-class positions (as a secretary and electrician). However, it is evident to me now that positive educational ideologies were always present in our household and our family's funds of knowledge influenced my own parents' attitudes and expectations of my educational experiences.
>
> (Kiyama, 2008, p. 21)

Within the dissertation I went on to share specific examples of the ways in which funds of knowledge manifested in my family. For example, although neither of my parents had officially been taught to navigate school systems, there were certain expectations around education for my siblings and me. College was not the goal; college was the expectation. Our local community college offered a summer experience, "College for Kids." I attended while in elementary school and was introduced at a very young age to a college campus. Just recently my mom excitedly informed me that my daughter would soon be old enough to attend as well. The idea of becoming a college student is a special process in my family.

Just a few years ago, when my grandmother, who lived with us until I was nine years old when she then moved into her own little home next door, passed away, I watched funds of knowledge come to life within the ranch community where I grew up. Our ranch is situated in what used to be a copper mining town and now has a population of less than 1,500, a small town that inevitably creates a sense of familism and closeness. Immediately after her passing, community members began dropping off food at the ranch, friends coordinated and cooked the lunch that was to be served at the church hall following my grandmother's services, and people sent my family money to help cover the costs of the services.

I was overwhelmed by the generosity and care that friends in our little town demonstrated. It was a clear illustration of the ways in which communities come together to lift one another up in times of need. These practices embody what I aim to demonstrate in my service roles. I actively resist the notion that individual benefit should take precedence over community need. My ranch knowledge has taught me that you share resources with others, you use your privilege to move aside and at times force others to listen to the long-standing cultural knowledge present in underserved communities, and you create opportunities for others along the way. My ranch knowledge has guided the way in which I serve and has blurred the lines between service in the academy and service in my community.

Serving My Community

It has been well documented that associate professors often have the heaviest teaching and service roles and that full professors have access to service roles that hold more value and prestige (see O'Meara et al., 2017 for a comprehensive review of the literature on this topic). As a tenured associate professor, I have certainly felt the heavy load of service. Recently I transitioned into the role of department chair, a leadership position that presumably is viewed as more high profile and more "in line" with my institution. Yet I find myself questioning the response I am supposed to have to this "valued" and "valuable" service role. I also find assumptions are made by others that an administrative or leadership position should be the next stage in my academic career (again see O'Meara et al., 2017 for a more in-depth discussion). And yet I find myself struggling to find congruence between the perceived value of the role, assumptions about my career trajectory, and my own intuition of service. I was concerned that I would become consumed by administrative tasks and begin neglecting the scholarship that I love, scholarship that has connected me with local underserved communities since before I began on a research trajectory. As one might guess, I reluctantly took on the role of department chair and soon came a congratulatory text from a close friend, my very first college friend who is also a first-generation Mexican. We grew up in neighboring copper mining towns and have supported one another's educational and professional pursuits for over twenty years. Upon sharing my reluctance, he messaged me,

> But you HAVE to do this. You know that. . .
> That's great for you and for all of the little Mexican girls and boys,
> The people from little towns,
> Immigrants,
> The list goes on. . .
> So proud of you!

His text was a gentle reminder that service within the academy, although perceived as individual leadership growth and contributions to the institution, is and has always been about offering a reconstructed image of what is possible for my community. Indeed the overall orientation of my work, which entwines research, teaching, and service, has always been externally focused. I often say, "The community should be our guide." Thus, my service is driven not by the institution that employs me nor to the professional field, but to the underserved communities who have long taught me how to fight for equitable educational opportunities. I aim to transform such spaces.

In previous work (Kiyama, 2018), I described this as a value in relationship- and trust-building between researchers and practitioners. The value centers community-driven or grassroots efforts. "Collaborations can start with members of the community. Grassroots efforts then drive the relationship and collaborative development by identifying and informing the efforts" (Kiyama, 2018, p. 41). And while I take seriously my commitment to the faculty, staff, and students in our department, I take my cues from our community partners when considering how we can leverage our departmental resources to impact educational opportunities. For me, community knowledge is as important as academic knowledge. They are not mutually exclusive. And I return to my friend's text message, which reminds me of the ease with which our histories and cultures are omitted and why our physical presence is so necessary. My physical presence in this role is an act of hope and solidarity.

Leslie

As someone who studies academic careers, I read and learned about the idea "community of scholars" early on in my graduate student career

(Goodman, 1962). Those papers described idyllic times in which professors came together to debate, to generate interesting new ideas, and to move their fields forward. Growing up in a family that often debated politics over dinner and holiday visits, the vision excited and inspired me—until it didn't. One day, while writing up a literature review, I realized that the community of scholars that I read about was never intended for me, a woman of color. Nor was it intended for anyone who was not wealthy, white, and male. I was—and am not—any of those things.

I grew up in a working-class home, where my dad worked in a meatpacking plant and my mom sporadically worked in nursing homes, caring for people about whom the rest of the world seemed to forget. We were living far away from our families in a small farming town in northern Texas, where my dad and all of his brothers had worked as seasonal farmworkers throughout their childhood and youth. Eventually the racism that I experienced in school and the loneliness of being far from family compelled my parents to move us back to northern New Mexico. We moved back to "the ranch," where many of my dad's brothers live within a five-mile radius, where branding the cows and cleaning the cattle guards served as mini-family reunions. My mom's family was just about forty minutes away, and weekends often meant gathering at my grandma's to go grocery shopping as a family and maybe a dinner out at my grandma's favorite restaurant, Kentucky Fried Chicken.

Although I don't think I realized it at the time, these family get-togethers were not only special and fun times, but they provided some of the greatest lessons of my life or, as Judy described them earlier in this chapter, as funds of knowledge anchored in my family's labor and cultural histories. From my dad's family, I learned about the importance of caring for the land and how to care for cattle when droughts ensued. I learned about the preservation of water, and most importantly I learned that the valuable work of people's hands is always informed by careful thought and analysis.

For example, recently my dad told me how my grampa would carefully count the rows of fields that he and his children would work and how he set up the siblings to cover as much ground as possible or to extend the work as long as he could depending on the farm owners' pay scale. From my mom's family, I learned how to really show up and love people, even when you are tired and do not have many resources. For instance, as my grandma aged, my mom would take my grandma to the doctor, the store, or Sonic for a shake even after working a grueling fifty-hour week. And no matter what, my grandma would always use her well-earned but meager food stamp allocation to buy snacks for her grandchildren.

Now as an adult, I draw on these experiences in all of my roles, especially as an advisor/mentor. For example, I find that I draw on the notions and habits of leadership modeled by my parents and especially my grandmothers. I had a small window of opportunity to watch both of my grandmothers—women with no formal education—manage large families with little money. They wisely managed through math, logistical precision, communication, and of course love. Today I use these skills to guide my work with students.

Unfortunately the lessons and knowledges gifted to me by my family don't show up in the academy or its valuation of people. Instead, as Judy noted earlier, it is typical for success and progression to be measured by individual advancement, and Bierema (2009) argues that these measures and narratives of success reinforce and are reinforced by white, patriarchal, and capitalistic logics. Subsequently the kinds of knowledges and lessons that communities of color and working-class communities bring into academia are viewed skeptically, subjected to harsh critique, and set aside as marginal, which leads me to my orientation to service. Below, I describe how I strive to act on service as I move into my post-tenure career.

Building a Community for Radical Possibility

Within the window of just one year, I have been presented with many service opportunities. Some of the service requests were framed as a way to "move my university forward in terms of diversity." Others have been framed as ways to "give back to my department." I have contemplated and taken on many, but not all, of these requests. For example, I promised myself that I will no longer serve as "diversity" for my institution. What I mean by this is that I refuse to save my institution by agreeing to serve on committees that are looking for a person of color. I have also decided that I will only engage in diversity work if diversity is to be followed by investments into inclusion and equity. Thus, ultimately, many of the commitments I *do* take up are not represented by my—or any—university's evaluative systems, but instead guided by a simple question, "How will this work allow me to work toward radical possibility?", which I envision as a broader, more inclusive community of scholars, one that invites and values the contributions of historically underrepresented scholars, especially women of color.

Specifically it is not uncommon for me to receive a text message or email from a student, especially students of color and particularly women, who want to know if I have time to "process." Sometimes these women want to process dissertation struggles; other times they need to process yet another experience of racialized sexism or straight-up racism that they have experienced in the context of a class or in an interaction with a peer. Other times, these women need to process how their family and academic lives seem to be falling apart or happily coming together at the same time.

To be frank, the texts do not always come at the most convenient time. I might be tired after a day of attending meetings, teaching, or negotiating the responsibilities of work and home. However, I hear the words of my dad, "Don't forget where you came from," and I think of how my mom and grandmothers managed so many more difficulties with fewer resources than I have. And so I have them over to the house, cook them a meal, and ask them to process their thinking as I cook. I have found that sharing a meal and thinking together is one of the best ways forward, and it models my belief that knowers and knowledge making are everywhere, just as my grandmothers modeled for me.

Interestingly this is also how many of the most important lessons and insights were passed onto me. My mom taught me to read and write while I snacked on cookies and milk, while always sitting at our small kitchen table. My dad and his entire family exchange the best family stories over family meals. To this end, at the beginning of each academic year, my family and I invite all of my advisees to our home for a meal of tacos and tostadas and salsa. Over the holiday break, it is quite typical for students to join us because I know the pain of living away from family during the holiday season. During these meals, we share stories about our family and college. We talk about our favorite music and movies. And we talk about how to navigate higher education, deal with difficult situations, frame letters of application, and prepare for the job market.

Of course, my institution, like most, has no check box for this kind of work, and in fact, my institution might like me to maintain a stricter boundary between personal and professional spaces. However, when I think about service, the most important forms of engagement are immeasurable and have little to do with committee work or formal leadership roles. Indeed my only reason for participating in such conventional service roles is because I understand that it will connect me to conversations and resources that are critical to laying or defending the groundwork for radical possibility. Indeed I recently agreed to serve as a program-level administrator, not because I am interested in serving my institution, but because I will be positioned to participate in many conversations related to student access and curriculum.

Looking Forward, Together

Through many conversations, we have reflected on our disposition to service and identified three critical points. First, service for both of us is driven by a need to act toward a collective purpose, and relatedly, our service commitments bend strongly toward the historically underserved communities that we are a part of and that have taught us so much. This orientation to serve our community rather than our institutions or professional fields is not prominent in formal institutional policy and discourse. Second, our understanding and engagement in service is deeply connected to the production and creation of knowledge. This means we refuse to privilege formal academic spaces as the only places where knowers and knowledge making take place. Third and relatedly, service, as we define it, is difficult to capture or measure. In fact, we have struggled to even articulate our approach and how empowering it feels to be in a position to serve, so we want to close with the following quotes, which summarize what we aim to do in our service work.

> It is in our joining together that we challenge "exclusion by collectively creating counter-spaces of cultural citizenship" in academia. "That is, [our] resistance [is] linked to a collective claim to space rights within the university."
> (Bañuelos, 2006, p. 99)

Conclusion

We wrote this chapter with women of color in mind, especially Latinas who might see a little of themselves in the cultural histories and counter-narratives we shared. It is important to us to close this work by providing strategies and pointers for post-tenure Latinas who are grappling with decisions related to service. We also find it important to provide concrete advice for institutional leaders whom are tasked with faculty work time allocations, faculty development, and evaluation.

It is appropriate and probably not surprising that many of these considerations were developed collectively. Specifically we recently attended an annual writing retreat with six other women of color. We affectionately refer to ourselves as, *Mujeres Xingonas*.[2] Dinners with these women served as a space to seek advice and share our triumphs and fears. As we shared our ideas for this chapter, stories about service and mentoring began to flow. Guided by that conversation and our own cultural histories, intuitions, and knowledges, we offer the following points for consideration.

For Your Consideration

1. *Mentoring amongst women of color is culturally informed, and it often exceeds formal or strictly academic matters.* Develop strategies to "track" these kinds of activities. For example, we have chosen to "code" all of our mentoring meetings in our academic calendars.
2. *Knowledge is created in the community.* We noted above our assumption that service is connected with knowledge production. In writing about culturally relevant pedagogies, Brockenbrough (2016) urges that we must consider pedagogical strategies enacted across the multiple contexts in which students live—social, communal, and educational. Thus, culturally relevant knowledge is not confined to school settings (Brockenbrough, 2016). We have established the argument that service is a space or an opportunity where knowledge making is possible. Find ways to describe how your scholarly work and service benefit one another or how your service is connected to the scholarly

work of your advisees. Also consider framing your service work as "community-engaged scholarship" or in language that might be more familiar to your university.
3. *Similarly we argue that in serving, we are learning from communities and producing knowledge in culturally relevant ways with our communities.* Elenes' (2006) description of border/transformative pedagogy, which is informed by Chicana feminist practices, summarizes this point well:

> Border/transformative practices offer a cultural critique of material conditions of subaltern communities that involve politics of change to transform society in order to become truly democratic. . . . They blur many distinctions artificially created in cultural productions and classroom practices.
>
> (p. 247)

Thus, service transcends and transforms traditional academic and disciplinary boundaries (Elenes, 2006). Find ways to discuss how your service is informing your thinking in your research and teaching. Map lessons that you have learned from the community onto your class syllabi or research agenda.

4. *Service is about transformation.* Transformation is difficult; it requires that we take care of ourselves in order to persist, so it is key to set intentions, as described below.

> An offering of intentions to those who have come before us and those to follow:
> We offer you these words
> We hope they will resonate with your own experiences
> May they remind you of your own power
> Give you the courage to heal and be your whole self
> Radiate the warmth and light you need to integrate bodymindspirit;
> Challenge yourself to
> Bold transgressions
> As you step over the imposed borders in work and life
> Because we are making nuestra historia
> Every step of the way.
>
> (Ayala, Herrera, Jiménez, and Lara, 2006, p. 277)

For University Administrators

We close this chapter with advice for chairs, deans, and faculty developers. Above all, we want to stress that women of color are likely to be carrying service loads that are larger, but perhaps more invisible, than others in your departments (O'Meara et al., 2017). Study after study has shown that women, particularly women of color, serve as informal mentors to students of color, including students not enrolled in the faculty person's program.

1. It is critical to *develop systems that are capable of tracking and rewarding such complex service workloads*, and in doing so, confer with women of color as to how best to capture the service work in which they are engaging.
2. *Realize that women of color are often looking for culturally informed mentoring* or mentoring that entails both academic and personal dimensions. Consider investing in programs that allow women of color to identify a mentor with whom they want to work rather than to assign them a mentor who may not be their best fit.
3. *Revise faculty evaluation policies and then invest in faculty development and training efforts that recognize the importance of service* and its connectedness to teaching, research, and student advancement, especially when service does not stem from formal institutional activities or assignments.

And so we urge you, look forward—with collective purpose and radical possibility.

Notes

1 Holling, Fu, and Bubar (2012, p. 265).
2 We extend our gratitude to Andrea Romero, Brandy Piña Watson, Marla Franco, Amanda Tachine, Ada Wilkinson-Lee, and Lucy Soltero for their support and ideas as we developed this chapter.

References

Ayala, J., Herrera, P., Jiménez, L., and Lara, I. (2006). Fiera, Guambra, y Karichina! In D. Delgado Bernal, C. A. Elenas, F. E. Godinez, and S. Villenas (Eds.), *Chicana/Latina education in everyday life: Feminista perspectives on pedagogy and epistemology* (pp. 261–280). Albany, NY: State University of New York Press.

Baez, B. (2000). Race-related service and faculty of color: Conceptualizing critical agency in academe. *Higher Education*, 39(3), 363–391.

Bañuelos, L. E. (2006). "Here they go again with the race stuff": Chicana negotiations of the graduate experience. In D. Delgado Bernal, C. A. Elenas, F. E. Godinez, and S. Villenas (Eds.), *Chicana/Latina education in everyday life: Feminista perspectives on pedagogy and epistemology* (pp. 95–112). Albany, NY: State University of New York Press.

Bierema, L. L. (2009). Critiquing human resource development's dominant masculine rationality and evaluating its impact. *Human Resource Development Review*, 8(1), 68–96.

Brockenbrough, E. (2016). Becoming queerly responsive: Culturally responsive pedagogy for Black and Latino urban queer youth. *Urban Education*, 51(2), 170–196.

Broido, E. M., Brown, K. R., Stygles, K. N., and Bronkema, R. H. (2015). Responding to gendered dynamics: Experiences of women working over 25 years at one university. *The Journal of Higher Education*, 86(4), 595–627.

Calderón, D., Delgado Bernal, D., Pérez Huber, L., Malagón, M., and Vélez, V. N. (2012). A Chicana feminist epistemology revisited: Cultivating ideas a generation later. *Harvard Educational Review*, 82(4), 513–539.

Delgado Bernal, D. (1998). Using a Chicana feminist epistemology in educational research. *Harvard Educational Review*, 68(4), 555–582.

Delgado-Bernal, D. (2007). La trenzas de identidades—Weaving together my personal, professional, and communal identities. In K. Gonzalez and R. Padilla (Eds.), *Doing the public good: Latina/o scholars engage civic participation* (pp. 135–149). Sterling, VA: Stylus Publishing, LLC.

Elenes, C. A. (2006). Transformando Fronteras: Chicana feminist transformative pedagogies. In D. Deldago Bernal, C. A. Elenes, F. E. Godinez, and S. Villenas (Eds.), *Chicana/Latina education in everyday life: Feminista perspectives on pedagogy and epistemology* (pp. 245–260). Albany, NY: State University of New York Press.

Elenes, C. A., and Delgado Bernal, D. (2010). Latina/o education and the reciprocal relationship between theory and practice: Four theories informed by the experiential knowledge of marginalized communities. In E. G. Murillo, Jr., S. A. Villenas, R. T. Galvan, J. S. Munoz, C. Martinez, and M. Machado-Casas (Eds.), *Handbook of Latinos and education: Theory, research and practice* (pp. 63–69). New York, NY: Routledge.

Holling, M. A., Fu, M. C., and Bubar, R. (2012). Dis/Jointed appointments: Solidarity amidst inequity, tokenism, and marginalization. In G. Gutiérrez y Muhs, Y. Flores Niemann, C. G. González, and A. P. Harris (Eds.), *Presumed incompetent: The intersections of race and class for women in academia* (pp. 250–265). Logan, UT: Utah State University Press.

Goodman, P. (1962). *The community of scholars*. New York, NY: Random House.

Gonzales, L. D. (2018). Subverting and minding boundaries: The intellectual work of women. *The Journal of Higher Education*, 89(5), 677–701.

Gutiérrez y Muhs, G., Flores Niemann, Y., González, C. G., and Harris, A. P. (2012). *Presumed incompetent: The intersections of race and class for women in academia*. Logan, UT: Utah State University Press.

Kiyama, J. M. (2008). *Funds of knowledge and college ideologies: Lived experiences among Mexican-American families* (Unpublished doctoral dissertation). The University of Arizona, Tucson, AZ.

Kiyama, J. M. (2018). Relationship and trust-building between researchers and practitioners: Toward educational equity for under-served populations (pp. 36–42). In H. T. Rowan-Kenyon, M. Cahalan, and M. Yamashita (Eds.), *Reflections on connecting research and practice in college access and success programs*. Washington, DC: Pell Institute for the Study of Opportunity in Higher Education.

Moll, L. C., Amanti, C., Neff, D., and Gonzalez, N. (1992). Funds of knowledge for teaching: Using a qualitative approach to connect homes and classrooms. *Theory into Practice*, 31(2), 132–141.

O'Meara, K., Kuvaeva, A., Nyunt, G., Waugaman, C., and Jackson, R. (2017). Asked more often: Gender differences in faculty workload in research universities and the work interactions that shape them. *American Educational Research Journal, 54*(6), 1154–1186.

Ward, K. (2003). *Faculty service roles and the scholarship of engagement: ASHE-ERIC higher education report—Jossey-Bass higher and adult education series.* New York, NY: Jossey-Bass Publications.

4 Developing Intentionality
How Postsecondary Institutions Can Nurture Latina Faculty Members to Achieve Tenure and Promotion

Edlyn Peña

In an article published by *The Chronicle of Higher Education* in the summer of 2018, "How Serious are you about Diversity Hiring?" Tugend (2018) interrogated California Lutheran University's (Cal Lutheran) history of cultural and structural barriers that contributed to the marginalization of faculty of color. One Cal Lutheran faculty member whom Tugend interviewed for the article lamented that faculty of color at Cal Lutheran were "hypervisible when they needed us to be in glossy brochures and invisible when it came to our needs" (para. 2). The voices of faculty of color whose needs had long been unmet began to reverberate across the campus, ultimately reaching the ears of Cal Lutheran's leadership team. Cal Lutheran's dated approaches to hiring, retention, and promotion of faculty of color compelled campus leaders to take major steps to redress the inequities. This chapter documents the institutional and cultural shifts that occurred to nurture the success and tenure of faculty of color, particularly female Latina faculty members. Using an autoethnographic methodological approach, I juxtapose my personal experiences as a Latina faculty member who successfully achieved tenure and promotion at Cal Lutheran with the structural and cultural factors that both challenged and facilitated this achievement.

By situating my personal narrative within the context of an evolving organizational culture, I examine the institution's role in developing what Tugend (2018) called *intentionality* among institutional leaders to support the recruitment, advancement, and tenure of Latina faculty members. "That intentionality," explained Tugend, "entails rewriting recruitment ads, training search committees with evidence-based research on how to avoid falling back into the status quo, and understanding why the process doesn't end with the hire" (para. 9).

The idea is that developing institutional practices with equitable outcomes in mind can lead to organizational change in predominantly white intellectual spaces. In this autoethnography, I frame the implications of my experiences from perspectives in organizational change and leadership (Adserias et al., 2016), as well as agentic perspectives within gendered organizations (O'Meara, 2015). In particular, I explore the intermingling of my personal experiences as a tenure-track Latina faculty member with institutional practices that involve honoring *familismo* (De Luca and Escoto, 2012), cultivating Latina faculty leaders while avoiding the threat of cultural taxation (Joseph and Hirshfield, 2011), and providing institutionalized supports and policies for Latina faculty to achieve tenure and promotion (Fleming, Goldman, Correll, and Taylor, 2016). These factors collectively played a part in my journey toward becoming a tenured faculty member. The implications of these experiences apply to the ways in which other Latina faculty members can navigate institutional culture and structures in U.S. postsecondary institutions. On a broader scale, the autoethnographic narrative represented in this chapter is instructive for institutions who wish to support the promotion and tenure of Latina faculty through leadership and policy changes.

Familismo

Cal Lutheran is a small, liberal arts college in southern California. Founded in 1959, the university continues to remain small and enrolls over 4,000 students in undergraduate and graduate programs. On my first day as an assistant professor in the Higher Education Leadership doctoral program at Cal Lutheran, I was plagued with worry and anxiety. It was fall 2009, and I had joined the ranks of a small handful of Latina tenure-track faculty members on campus. At that time, Cal Lutheran was considered a predominantly white institution, with low numbers of students of color and even lower numbers of faculty of color. Out of five people in my department, I was the only Latina, a common experience for female Latina faculty members at many universities (De Luca and Escoto, 2012). What would it be like for a young Latina woman like me to survive the tenure process at a predominantly white institution? My son, Diego, was only eighteen months old. I strove to achieve the elusive family-work balance people so often talked about. And elusive it was.

In my first semester, I prepared and taught three new courses. I was assigned to chair six doctoral dissertations. These responsibilities firmly required me to devote a minimum of fifty hours a week to my faculty position. I quietly made attempts to adjust, some days finding great joy in my work with doctoral students, other days lamenting the lost hours I could not seem to recover with Diego. How could I, a new Latina faculty member, prove my worthiness—my capacity to earn tenure—at a predominantly white institution while managing the increasing demands of motherhood?

During my first year engaged as a faculty member, I began to notice striking changes in Diego's developmental trajectory. I slowly became aware that some of Diego's behaviors decreased or disappeared altogether between the ages of one to two years old. Why was he no longer responding to his name? What happened to the few words he spoke at the brink of turning one? Where had Diego's eye contact gone? By the end of my first fall semester at Cal Lutheran, I reached out to medical professionals for assessments and answers. After a number of doctor's visits, my husband and I received the news in the middle of the spring semester of 2010. Diego had autism.

How do I explain what it is like to receive this kind of news about your child? Your love for them never falters. In fact, your love for them grows. Your extended Latinx family may not necessarily know how to support you or your child with a disability, even when they have the desire to do so (Hughes, Valle-Riestra, and Arguelles, 2008). As you consider your child's future, your emotions begin to run deep, and your breath catches. You find it even more difficult to navigate the confusing maze of disability services while attempting to attend to your responsibilities on campus committees, faculty meetings, classes, and research. You begin to ask yourself, "How can I possibly attend to my child's ever-increasing needs given the great demands placed on me as a faculty member? What would it mean for a mother like me to thrive and earn tenure at a teaching institution that requires publications in peer-reviewed journals and great amounts of institutional service?"

I weighed the feasibility of providing early, intensive intervention for Diego within this context. Without question, addressing my son's diagnosis of autism would demand a tremendous amount of time beyond my fifty-hour workweek. In my mind, there was no question. Diego came first.

My motivation to choose my son over work was in many ways driven by *familismo*, a core Latinx value placed on family loyalty (De Luca and Escoto, 2012). *Familismo* is more specifically described as "family closeness, cohesion, and interdependence, an expectation and reliance on family members—including intergenerational and extended kin—as primary sources of instrumental and emotional support, and the commitment to the family over individual needs and desires" (Durand, 2011, p. 258). Within Latinx families, mothers in particular are often framed as the primary socialization agent responsible for structuring the family environment to support and maintain *familismo*. Latinx faculty members who have developed strong professional identities must navigate the tension between *familismo* and a faculty position that fulfills them professionally, financially, and emotionally. Given my past experiences with family-unfriendly research institutions, I was under the impression I had to choose between Diego and my faculty role.

When I approached my provost to discuss my situation and resign, I was met with a surprise. Rather than accepting my resignation from my faculty position to tend to Diego's needs, the provost encouraged me to work out a plausible way to retain me. She granted me a part-time family leave that lasted three years. I was also granted an extra year extension toward my tenure and promotion timeline. I quickly learned in this moment that an influential administrative leader, my provost, honored my value of *familismo*. Her support in allowing me to maintain the dual roles of mother and assistant professor in a manageable way signaled the intentionality that Cal Lutheran had to support me as a valued Latina member of the campus community. De Luca and Escoto (2012) explain that "if the organization is not supportive, Latinas might stop attempting to be included in a majority-dominated profession" (p. 33). Had the provost not made the pivotal decision to preserve my faculty role while allowing me to put family first, I would no longer be in a faculty position.

Avoiding Cultural Taxation

In the years that followed, I found that for the most part, my faculty and administrative colleagues supported me in my efforts to meet and exceed teaching, research, and service expectations. The difficulty I found in working at a small liberal arts college was that the institution depended heavily on service to the campus community. Further, my status as a Latina faculty member meant that Cal Lutheran administrators identified additional areas in which I could serve in leadership positions to support the institution's commitment to students of color. I later learned that I was not alone in experiencing increased expectations to address diversity-related institutional efforts. This phenomenon is known as *cultural taxation* (Padilla, 1994), described as a burden in which "additional responsibilities are placed upon non-white faculty because of their ethnoracial backgrounds" (Joseph and Hirshfield, 2011, p. 121). In their study of faculty of color, Joseph and Hirshfield (2011) document the many in ways in which faculty are tapped on the shoulder to take on extra commitments due to their minority status on campus. When faculty of color are overburdened or overcommitted to additional responsibilities, such as serving on diversity committees and mentoring students of color, they experience cultural taxation. Consequently faculty members can experience differential rates of work-related stress compared to white colleagues (Joseph and Hirshfield, 2011).

After beginning to feel burned out in my faculty role at Cal Lutheran, I was forced to learn how to circumnavigate the threat of cultural taxation resulting from institutional service. I reflected on the potential consequences of saying no to additional requests for labor that were oftentimes uncompensated. For instance, as I describe in the section below, Cal Lutheran institutionalized a policy to assign faculty "equity advocates" to all faculty search committees. Equity advocates are trained faculty members who serve on search committees to encourage the committee to consider equity issues in decision-making processes. The priority is to increase the recruitment and retention of faculty of color, including Latinas. Being identified and trained to become an equity advocate with a select group of faculty members was indeed an honor. At the same time, I found that engaging in a yearlong training process with the intention of serving on at least one faculty search committee each year that followed was quite a time commitment.

To be fair, Cal Lutheran did pay equity advocates to be trained in their first year of involvement. The remaining years of service were considered part of service requirements to the university. The year after I was trained to be an equity advocate, the provost's office asked me to chair a search committee and also serve on a second search committee as an equity advocate. Anyone who has served on a search committee understands the hours of labor that goes into recruiting, reviewing, interviewing, and hiring a faculty candidate. After serious consideration, I politely declined to participate in a second search committee.

Learning to say no, especially for Latina faculty, is certainly no easy feat. I sometimes made these decisions through trial and error. For instance, when the diversity office on campus asked me to serve as mentor to students of color, I agreed for one year. The next year I decided I could not add one more thing to my plate, and when asked to serve as a mentor again, I said no. In other cases, the importance of declining to participate in a major activity was clear to me. For example, when a vice president at Cal Lutheran asked me to serve on a HSI grant committee that would require heavy lifting, I had just accepted the role of directing the doctoral program in education, which was a major administrative task. I respectfully declined the invitation. To be clear, it took me years to muster the courage to set boundaries like this. After feeling myself burning out with service commitments, I weighed the benefits and consequences of this kind of decision against what it would mean for achieving tenure and promotion. This was my way of engaging agency to avoid cultural taxation.

While I make sense of cultural taxation in terms of racialized experiences, these very experiences also occurred within a gendered context. Like most historically predominantly white institutions, Cal Lutheran was founded and run by white men. Until recently, leadership positions were dominated by men, and their decisions and policy-making impacted women and minority faculty. Even the messages communicated had the potential to be gendered—such as the time one of my former male deans referred to me as "the good wife." These intersectional experiences of race and gender manifest as accumulated disadvantages, a burden that Latina faculty members often bear. In her research on the experiences of women faculty, O'Meara (2015) sheds light on the decision-making process women faculty make through the lens of personal agency within gendered organizations. In light of balancing family and work responsibilities, women learn "to evaluate these barriers in light of their specific goals and design responses. In other words, they needed to enact a form of agency, and that is what they did" (p. 352). O'Meara describes this experience as developing agentic perspectives. "These perspectives," she explained, "enhanced the sense of control [women faculty] felt and helped them to focus and prioritize in career contexts that were often ambiguous and project themselves into the future" (p. 352). As such, Latina women not only learn to identify and address additional requests placed on them because of their status as faculty of color to avoid cultural taxation, they also learn to negotiate the additional challenges they encounter as women in institutions whose leadership is oftentimes overrepresented by men. It likely comes as no surprise to Latina faculty in the trenches that female faculty of color are often forced to navigate "personal and psychological minefields" (Ruffins, 1997, p. 21) as they balance stress in their academic and personal lives. Weighing institutional assignments, declining participation, and negotiating boundaries are all forms of agency and coping mechanisms that enable Latina faculty to persist in organizations with unequal expectations placed on them.

Institutionalized Supports for Latina Faculty

While developing agentic perspectives is certainly important for the survival of Latina faculty members, we must not forget the responsibility that postsecondary institutions bear in creating more equitable environments for Latina faculty. With great effort, organizations can become responsive, welcoming, and inclusive to Latina faculty. When I first arrived at Cal Lutheran, there was little focus on creating these kinds of environments for faculty of color. Though my colleagues were largely supportive, I oftentimes felt isolated and did not have a Latina faculty mentor to which I could turn.

The beginnings of a cultural shift at Cal Lutheran occurred in the years leading up to 2016 when it received the HSI federal designation. By that point, over 25 percent of the student population was Latinx, but were not graduating at equal rates to their white student counterparts. The university president and provost began to pivot with regard to its commitment to serving Latinx students and other students of color. Cal Lutheran's leadership realized that, in order to meet the needs of its increasingly diverse student body, the organization needed to change. Yet the kind of change that would be meaningful to providing equitable opportunities to students of color needed to be a deep kind of change in terms of the organization's "underlying values or mission, culture, functioning processes, and structure of the organization" (Kezar, 2001, p. 16).

One of the more important ways the university decided to amplify its support for the retention and persistence of Latinx students was to hire and support more Latinx faculty and other faculty of color. The premise behind this effort was that a more proportionate representation of faculty of color would provide a greater pool of instructors, advisors, and mentors to support students from Latinx backgrounds. More

Latinx faculty representation had the potential to bridge the cultural gap between Latinx students and a historically predominantly white institution. In addition, the burden of cultural taxation might be reduced by distributing the work by hiring more faculty of color.

Cal Lutheran's president and provost brought in consultants from the Center for Urban Education at University of Southern California to engage Cal Lutheran in an institutional self-analysis of faculty hiring and retention practices (Bensimon, 2018). In the *Chronicle of Higher Education* article described at the beginning of this chapter, Tugend (2018) detailed the kind of work involved in this process. Faculty members, mostly of color, were nominated and invited to serve on an evidence team by the provost. Team meetings encouraged faculty members to reflect on their experiences as faculty of color and ways the institution could improve policies and practices centered on faculty hiring and retention. In his article, Tugend quoted the provost to describe the deep, reflective conversations in which the evidence team engaged:

> During their evidence-team meetings, 'nonwhite faculty started sharing their experience of what it was like to be a person of color here, and it was eye-opening,' says Neilson. 'We had some deep emotional types of conversations, but I would say in general, outside the evidence team, I don't think faculty of color felt comfortable talking about their experiences.' She'd always thought of the university as 'a very pleasant and nice place' and wasn't aware that some of her colleagues did not. 'I had my blinders on,' she says.

These sorts of conversations clearly impacted the provost, enabling her to question the norms and values of the institution. From these conversations, our evidence team began to examine and deconstruct Cal Lutheran's faculty search guidelines. Evidence team members turned into equity advocates. And those equity advocates were empowered by Cal Lutheran's leadership to uphold new policies and practices in equitable hiring and supportive retention practices. I was honored to be a part of this institutional change effort that ultimately resulted in hiring greater numbers of faculty of color, including Latina faculty.

In addition to recruiting more faculty of color, Cal Lutheran committed to providing mentoring and professional development for the faculty members of color they hired. The provost's office funded the participation of Latina faculty and other faculty of color in comprehensive professional development programs for tenure (Rockquemore, 2013). Cal Lutheran became an institutional member of the National Center for Faculty Development and Diversity. The provost's office invited assistant professors of color to submit proposals to participate in the center's Faculty Success Program for untenured faculty. The program involved individual mentoring from tenured faculty, structured faculty mentoring sessions, and professional development to amass strategies and tools to achieve tenure. I was honored to participate in this Faculty Success Program myself the year before I earned tenure. As a result of participating in that program, I refined my skills in setting healthy boundaries at work while increasing my scholarly productivity. That year alone, I was able to finish five journal articles. All five were eventually accepted for publication.

I want to underscore that the intentionality to support a Latina faculty like me was driven by the leadership of Cal Lutheran's president and provost after listening to the needs and interests of faculty of color. Scholars such as Adserias, Charleston, and Jackson (2017) emphasize the role of senior leaders in diversity and organizational change efforts. Deep and lasting transformation of organizational culture requires senior leaders—presidents, provosts, and other high-ranking administrators—to be engaged (Aguirre and Martinez, 2006). In fact, "more than any other factor, the leadership's commitment to deep and meaningful change will determine whether the institution builds capacity for the long-term" (Williams, 2013, p. 176). This is what strong institutional intentionality looks like.

An important consideration in this discussion is the fact that the change efforts described in this chapter were situated in the context of a small private college. Compared to public institutions or even large private research institutions, more bureaucracy, policies, and red tape can be encountered while accomplishing institutional change. Baker and Baldwin (2015) also note that liberal arts institutions are susceptible to organizational change. Factors such as addressing external forces (e.g., change in community demographics) and achieving equilibrium between the internal and external environments are documented as highly influencing organizational change in liberal arts institutions. Cal Lutheran itself was looking to create an equilibrium with regard to providing equitable opportunities for people of color from the community that translated to opportunities for the increasing diversity of Cal Lutheran students and the faculty. Given the small size of the faculty and student body, along with flexibility in changing policies such as faculty search criteria, administrative leaders arguably had more autonomy to advance the diversity agenda.

Strategic Implications

In this chapter, I situated my personal experiences within the sociocultural dynamics—both racialized and gendered—of my institution. While I faced a set of challenges in becoming accustomed to navigating the institutional culture at Cal Lutheran, I attribute institutional leaders' honoring *familismo*, the agency I enacted to circumvent cultural taxation, and the provision of institutional supports to achieve tenure as experiences that empowered me to thrive as a Latina in academia. These experiences can inform the actions of postsecondary leaders at other teaching institutions. To honor the family values of Latinas, institutions can be sensitive to family dynamics and challenges faced by Latina faculty when they arise. The families of these faculty members might be included or involved in institutional events and programs. Leaders can assist Latina faculty in avoiding cultural taxation by being mindful of not asking the faculty to engage in numerous diversity-related initiatives above and beyond their common workload. This, of course, may not be possible until more faculty of color are hired to distribute the workload. Until that happens, leaders can be intentional about identifying white faculty allies to participate in diversity and equity efforts. Lastly, institutions can develop policies and structures similar to the equity advocate initiative to improve the campus culture for hiring and retaining faculty of color. Leaders can fund and support mentoring and professional development programs for tenure-track Latina faculty such as the Faculty Success Program offered by the National Center for Faculty Development and Diversity.

Leaders are encouraged to consider the power they have to make organizational change. After all, cultural changes required to advance institutional diversity and equity agendas require strong leadership (Adserias et al., 2017). In historically predominantly white institutions like Cal Lutheran, leaders may consider hiring more Latinas in faculty positions to create stronger networks and mentors among faculty of color. Further, Latinas should be considered for leadership positions, such as department chairs, program directors, deans, and vice presidents. Creating a leadership development program for Latina faculty would demonstrate an even deeper commitment to cultivating equitable opportunities for Latinas to be a part of all levels of institutional decision-making. By increasing the number of Latina faculty on campus, junior Latina faculty will feel supported and welcomed. They will be encouraged to surround themselves with other Latina faculty and allies who have navigated the tenure process. Similarly, hiring a greater number of Latina faculty can result in students of color, especially Latinx students, feeling supported by a stronger network of faculty advisors and mentors. Latina faculty can also attempt to expand their networks to people who can empower them and inspire agentic perspectives. They can leverage these perspectives as navigational tools in environments that are inequitable (O'Meara, 2015).

In their analysis of leadership styles that promote organizational change to advance diversity agendas, Adserias et al. (2017) found that transformational leadership can be an effective approach. Transformational leadership involves planned and strategic changes in organizational culture. It interweaves principles of equity and social justice into the diversity agenda. Transformational change requires "leaders' ability to create and maintain relationships, create and communicate a vision of an inclusive and equitable campus and to inspire action in others"

(p. 326). Cal Lutheran's provost became intentional about improving the climate for faculty of color, communicating a vision on how to do that, and developing a web of support among faculty and administrators to achieve new organizational goals. Consequently, honest conversations ensued about inequities on campus, and real changes to hire and support a more diverse faculty were institutionalized. Cal Lutheran's administrators have made major improvements to keep this promise. The transformation in culture has enabled me to feel empowered to achieve tenure and promotion. In spring 2016, I successfully earned tenure and was promoted to associate professor. I am now one of a growing number of Latina faculty who will continue to thrive in higher education.

Thriving Post-Tenure

While achieving tenure and promotion is a major accomplishment, one's personal and professional development as a Latina faculty member does not end the moment tenure and promotion are granted. Latina faculty members should continue seeking support for growth and fulfillment while institutional leaders should simultaneously be mindful about continuing to support Latina faculty post-tenure.

After Diego was diagnosed with autism, I was blessed that Cal Lutheran supported me in pivoting my research agenda to understand the experiences of college students with autism. In 2010, when Diego was diagnosed, very little published research existed on the experiences of autistic students in higher education. My decision to change the trajectory of my research from supporting Latinx and black college students to supporting college students with autism was never challenged or questioned among my Cal Lutheran colleagues. I was free to explore this unchartered terrain without institutional or political barriers. My scholarly work turned into activism. My activism became deeply connected to preparing postsecondary institutions for students like Diego—namely, minimally verbal students with autism who use augmentative and alternative communication. This historically underserved student population seldom gained access to college programs, much less inclusion, in K-12 general education settings.

In 2016, I co-founded the Autism and Communication Center (ACC) with Cal Lutheran's president and board of regents' full endorsement. ACC has become a national resource center that empowers people with autism to choose and use alternative forms of communication to access inclusive school and community environments. The mission of ACC was shaped by Diego's personal experiences. Diego faced numerous obstacles in becoming included in general education and in accessing a robust communication system through a letter board and iPad. I advocated fiercely for Diego, and in turn, he learned to advocate for himself. He astutely explained to others what it was like to experience autism from his perspective. In fact, in 2017, Diego wrote a short nonfiction book as part of a school project in third grade. He titled the book, *Anatomy of Autism*. In the book, he described the various barriers he contends with in relation to his communication, motor planning, and sensory system. Upon reading the manuscript, Diego's third-grade teacher immediately encouraged us to publish the book. Within twenty-four hours of being released on Amazon, *Anatomy of Autism* became a number-one best seller. Diego and I have since co-presented at numerous schools, colleges, and national conferences. *Anatomy of Autism* has now been translated to Spanish and Portuguese, with a translated version in Hindi on its way. The success of Diego's book has been a wonderful surprise and blessing.

My scholarship informs my capacity to support Diego; likewise, Diego's experiences inform my scholarly and advocacy pursuits. The willingness of Cal Lutheran's leadership to support me in pursuing my passion on a personal and professional level is not taken for granted. Through our advocacy work, Diego and I continue to pave the way for a brighter future for autistic students. Collectively, our work has reached international audiences. Cal Lutheran's intentionality to support the development of a Latina faculty like me is what made this global impact possible.

References

Adserias, R. P., Charleston, L. J., and Jackson, J. F. (2017). What style of leadership is best suited to direct organizational change to fuel institutional diversity in higher education? *Race, Ethnicity and Education*, 20(3), 315–331.

Aguirre, Jr. A., and Martinez, R. O. (2006). Diversity leadership in higher education. *ASHE Higher Education Report*, 32(3). San Francisco, CA: Jossey-Bass.

Baker, V. L., and Baldwin, R. G. (2015). A case study of liberal arts colleges in the 21st century: Understanding organizational change and evolution in higher education. *Innovative Higher Education*, 40(3), 247–261.

Bensimon, E. M. (2018, March 26). Creating racially and ethnically diverse faculties. *Inside Higher Education*. Retrieved from www.insidehighered.com/views/2018/03/26/new-policies-are-needed-recruit-racially-and-ethnically-diverse-faculties-opinion

De Luca, S. M., and Escoto, E. R. (2012). The recruitment and support of Latino faculty for tenure and promotion. *Journal of Hispanic Higher Education*, 11(1), 29–40.

Durand, T. (2011). Latina mothers' cultural beliefs about their children, parental roles, and education: Implications for effective and empowering home-school partnerships. *Urban Review*, 43(2), 255–278.

Fleming, S., Goldman, A., Correll, S., and Taylor, C. (2016). Settling in: A qualitative study of factors contributing to new faculty network development. *Journal of Higher Education*, 87(4), 544–572.

Hughes, M. T., Valle-Riestra, D. M., and Arguelles, M. E. (2008). The voices of Latino families raising children with special needs. *Journal of Latinos and Education*, 7(3), 241–257.

Joseph, T. D., and Hirshfield, L. E. (2011). 'Why don't you get somebody new to do it?' Race and cultural taxation in the academy. *Ethnic and Racial Studies*, *34*(1), 121–141.

Kezar, A. (2001). Understanding and facilitating change in higher education in the 21st century: Recent research and conceptualizations. *ASHE Education Report*, *28*(4). San Francisco, CA: Jossey-Bass.

O'Meara, K. (2015). A career with a view: Agentic perspectives of women faculty. *Journal of Higher Education*, *86*(3), 331–359.

Padilla, A. M. (1994). Ethnic minority scholars, research, and mentoring: Current and future issues. *Educational Researcher*, *23*(4), 24–27.

Rockquemore, K. (2013, August 12). A mentoring manifesto. *Inside Higher Education*. Retrieved from www.insidehighered.com/advice/2013/08/12/essay-how-be-good-faculty-mentor-junior-professors

Ruffins, P. (1997). The fall of the house of tenure. *Black Issues in Higher Education*, *14*(7), 19–26.

Tugend, A. (2018, June 10). How serious are you about diversity hiring? *The Chronicle of Higher Education*. Retrieved from www.chronicle.com/article/How-Serious-Are-You-About/243684

Williams, D. A. (2013). *Strategic diversity leadership*. Sterling, VA: Stylus Publishers, LLC.

5 Reflections on Becoming a Full Professor
A Journey Best Walked Together

Julie López Figueroa

While the tenure process and review vary slight depending on one's institutional system, hearing firsthand the common concerns and sometimes worries voiced by graduate students and junior faculty in various, unrelated venues, coupled with the demographic underrepresentation of Latinas in higher education, makes this book timely and critical. To illustrate, in December 2017, the Faculty Employment Report from the California State University (CSU) Chancellor's Office identified 2,129 female full professors within the system. Disaggregating Latina full professors across the CSU system, we are rendered with 197 across the system. At Sacramento State, I represent one of thirteen Latina full professors on my campus. Keeping these numbers in mind, perhaps one key challenge to pursuing tenure can be the way tenure is framed.

Typically each junior faculty receives a manual describing what evidence to insert or upload for review during probationary years leading up to tenure and post-tenure reviews. During the probationary post-tenure review years, one is required to submit evidence that speaks to all four or three of the following categories: research, scholarship, service, and teaching. Reflecting on my tenure process from a professor lens, two key challenges stood out for me. First, I believed the tenure process demanded innovation and excellence, but with time another reality surfaced. Addressing predetermined criteria in my file from one year to the next began to make this process formulaic, at best. When you realize the kind of transformative work required to create greater access for Chicana/o and Latina/o communities in higher education, for example, then the last thing you want to do is become formulaic in your thinking and practice. Even though my reviews were strong, the practice of preparing my file from one year to the next surfaced tenets that could be associated with social reproduction and individualism. In other words, the excellence demanded by the communities we study exceeded the expectations of what could fully be accounted for in the tenure process. And second, the culture of practice of self-promotion in reflective or professional development statements promotes the dishonest notion that one's success singularly manifest and results from the ability to be self-made. It hardly seems realistic to speak comfortably about being self-made without acknowledging the important contributions of our families, communities, friends, mentors, research participants, staff, students, and others that enable us to succeed in our work. There is a real tension between the culture of practice to attain tenure and the culture of practice of being Latina faculty. Mindful of these two challenges, this chapter primarily seeks to offer assurances about how acquiring tenure is as much about working productively to meet identified criteria as it is about intimately understanding what it takes to do your best work. What approaches can be considered useful in the pursuit of being promoted to full professor?

My goals for this chapter are three-fold. First, the chapter begins by discussing how early family experiences anchored me as a person and ultimately framed the mind-set that I rely on not just on my pursuit of tenure. Second, I highlight the kinds of networks and mentoring that positioned me to thrive through each tenure review, which are indispensable to work the politics surrounding tenure. Third, I want to shed some light on what being a professor means in my professional and personal life. Finally I want to share a list of helpful guidelines to remember that were co-constructed with my good friend and colleague, Dr. Gloria M. Rodriguez, that perhaps offer policy implications on how to best support graduate students and junior faculty. This chapter speaks to several themes: service from a stance of abundance, critical inquiry around success, the role of mentors/mentoring, resisting the status quo, the importance of support networks, and well-being.

As a professor, the academic training I received as a doctoral student from the University of California, Berkeley, within the School of Education prepared me to meet the academic rigor and expectations associated with tenure. However, the tenacity and fortitude that carried me through the tenure process did not entirely come from my time in academia. Rather, holding onto my humanity, dignity, and values through tenure happened as a result of lived experiences outside the academy. As a professor, my successful tenure reviews resulted from weaving academic and nonacademic experiences to inspire a practice of reciprocity and gratitude. In terms of the academy, networking practices and mentoring opportunities successfully positioned me to develop a solid practice to strike a personal/professional balance to thrive within an often-dehumanizing academic context. As for nonacademic experiences, the lessons experienced or witnessed growing up in my home and community were powerfully influential. The cumulative impact of these experiences gave me permission to embrace that as a first-generation professor there would be nothing typical about my path to and through tenure.

Living in the Realm of Possibility and Abundance

Intentionality is something I infuse into my practice as a professor given how I witnessed it as a child. Growing up in San José, California, I was raised by two Mexican immigrant and migrant parents, Maria and Macedonio. Soon after the birth of their third child (me), my parents decided to settle in San José, California, working in the local canneries. Whereas my father lacked the opportunity to attend school he eventually learned to read by the time he was 17 years old, my mother attended school up to the sixth grade and then trained to become a typist. Although my parents worked hard, a limited education dictated where we could afford to live as a family. And even though we lived below the poverty line, my parents' dreams were too big and steadfast for their children to be confined to any neighborhood. My neighborhood was beautifully complicated. The daily violence, gang activities, or drug use that often took place coexisted with the undeniable presence of loving and hardworking families. By definition we were poor, and though we had very few luxuries, my parents committed to offset our daily experiences by planning our future in very distinct ways.

My parents supported a curiosity for learning and instilled a consciousness about making a positive difference for others in the world. Even with very limited financial resources, my parents still found ways to hold sacred our childhood and intentionally direct our attention toward possibility. My parents always taught us to live by values and not ego, so without a second thought, one of my parents stood in line each Christmas so we might receive gifts from Salvation Army. They thought of our childhood more than their pride. On the exceptional occasion when gifts were purchased, it was commonplace for my sister, two brothers, and I to share one gift. As children we received a Spanish-English dictionary, and I also recollect my folks brought home a used desk to establish a dedicated space for us to do our homework. Though we lived in a three-bedroom apartment, my parents chose to place both set of bunk beds in the same room. The unoccupied room served as a playroom. In fact, I remember my dad found a discarded tabletop. While my mom cleaned it really well, my dad drove to a local hardware store and purchased legs to attach to the bottom of the tabletop. Before the day's end, we had a table whose surface was used to lay out the butcher paper (my parents asked for extra butcher paper from the butcher). We used the table to draw on or play with playdoh. We made up games, listened to music, and learned to draw in that room. Beyond gifts, my parents scheduled activities such as naptime, chores, and planned outings to free days at the local museums. We kept the dates for the mobile library accessible, visited California missions, took day trips to the ocean, and watched a lot of PBS.

During my elementary school years, I remember my mom—with assistance of a staff person translating for my mom in English—being head of the PTA at my school. She organized parents, advocated for children, and challenged the misconception that teachers sometimes held about the children and families who lived in our neighborhood. To support my mother's school involvement, my father took on any cooking and transportation responsibilities. My dad made breakfast and dinner at the same time, and they both shared doing our family's laundry. I developed a sense that my parents were a team.

In fact, I also remember my father prioritized taking my mother to the Indian Health Center (IHC) of Santa Clara Valley to learn about community resources and nutrition. On Sunday evenings, I remembered my parents sat in the living room on the couch listening to a Javier Solis (Mexican singer) record playing in the background. These Sunday evening discussions focused on the schedule for the coming week and what goals my parents wanted to accomplish for our family. While we played at their feet, my parents discussed how important it was to attend IHC workshops, decided which park we would visit the next time, confirmed the hours for the mobile library, and reviewed our family's financial budget for the week. Whether my mother was attending an IHC workshop, leading a PTA meeting, or volunteering at school, my father happily agreed to drive her to where she needed to go because my mother never learned to drive. Because my father considered my mother as a partner, it was not difficult for him to trust and support her intentions on how they were going to raise their children or live as a family.

The idea of being of service as a professor resonated with me given my upbringing. Growing up poor had its limitations, but I never lacked the basic essentials needed to live. In fact, my parents always lived with an orientation of abundance. For example, early in my childhood my parents collected bread and other grocery items from different local bakeries and stores to distribute from our living room for our hungry neighbors. When I attended UC Davis from 1987 to1992, I remember my parents brought care packages of some Mexican grocery basics for some friends whose parents were unable to visit Davis frequently. Let me say, we did not have a lot of money, but rice, beans, and tortillas along with some fresh vegetables always seemed financially affordable. To this day when I take my parents to run errands, it is more common than not my folks either will give a few dollars or buy a lunch for a stranger that looks like he or she needs help. Their thoughtfulness and generosity with strangers profoundly impacted my way of thinking about community. Needless to say, I witnessed my parents striving for excellence as parents and human beings through a narrative and practice that spoke to a collective well-being. Witnessing my parents structurally and dynamically negotiate the daily constraints of being poor and having a limited grasp of English taught me that faith is key to having success happen. You just need a plan and a support team. With this foundation, my version of succeeding in life starkly differed from the way I was being taught in school how to academically succeed.

While it might be a tendency to think of my parents as simply resilient or motivated, I invite readers to reframe this as persistence, resistance, self-determination, and self-advocacy. My parents' decision to forge a future while having access to few conventional resources translated into their becoming even more resourceful and creative. Because of their resourcefulness, resistance, and advocacy, my parents' consciousness about policy manifested from understanding the world from the margins. Existing policies such as those specifically addressing poverty, immigration, bilingualism, literacy, and housing impacted our well-being. Watching my parents advocate and work hard for their children to access a quality life and education meant they were also vigilant to question who benefits from existing policies. The process of questioning, responding, and resolving our living situation made me mindful to understand how policies and structures mediate one's quality of life, but they do not have the ultimate authority to squash one's agency and consciousness.

To this point, after the first two probationary reviews, I realized that tenure would not push me to the level of excellence that my community needed from me. Arrogance is not intended here. Rather the idea is that working beyond the limitations of predetermined criteria translates into having a more profound and meaningful tenure experience, which lays the foundation for promotion to full professor in a more self-determined manner.

Brokered Opportunities to Academically Succeed

From time to time, someone will ask if I always wanted to be a professor. Let me say that I never found school to be a welcoming space. I enjoyed learning, but I did not enjoy the kind of exchanges that seemed to invite argument or debate as a way of expressing intelligence and being able to hold one's ground. I never liked the competitive nature of school that was reflected in the amount of stars next to someone's name or the idea of winners and losers during the spelling bee on Fridays. So from the time I began Head Start all the way through high school, my stomach was a ball of nerves. I could never keep breakfast down knowing school awaited me. To further explain how I felt about school, many years later I realized that natural disasters such as earthquakes, hurricanes, and tornados captured my attention when it came to student's choice on written assignments. Keep this detail in mind for later.

While I scored pretty well on standardized exams in my early years of elementary school, my transition from elementary to middle school and middle school to high school was a different story. Post elementary school, the standardized exams in middle school and high school used to place me in the appropriate courses carved my pathway to being placed in special education. Though my time in special education totaled to about one year in middle school and my first year in high school, the damage was done. No matter how hard my parents tried to remind me I was smart, the evidence of my scores proved otherwise. This kind of hard evidence or measurement of success used in assessment somehow overrode the love and care my parents were compassionately offering me. I felt hopeless about my future, let alone about graduating and pursuing college until one day a teacher, Mrs. Musumecci, changed my life!

By the time the spring semester started of my ninth-grade year, I moved from writing book reports on natural disasters to writing about the *Titanic*. Essentially I wrote about a ship disaster as a metaphor for my life when I think about that book report. The scores on my assessment test placed me in a low-level English course. Up until this time, I felt like my lack of academic success resulted from something I failed to do or understand. However, feeling like a sinking ship did not last beyond two months after starting freshman year. My life changed one afternoon while I stayed after school to get extra help from my English teacher, Mrs. Maestas. Receiving help often meant writing on my own and asking for help if I were stuck on an idea, spelling of a word, or sentence structure.

During one of those days, Mrs. Maestas left to the front office to submit the attendance roster. I sat in the classroom alone editing the draft of my book report. I sat for at least half an hour when I heard the door—that interconnected the classrooms—on my right swung open. I saw Mrs. Musumecci walk through the door. She introduced herself and asked about the teacher's location. Once I explained my teacher went to the front office and said she'd be back, my focus returned to editing. I assumed Mrs. Musumecci was satisfied with my response and returned to her room, but instead she walked over to me, stood over my right shoulder, and asked what I was doing.

I glanced up and said, "I'm writing a book report on the *Titanic*."

Again I returned my focus to editing when a few seconds later she said, "Can make a copy of your book report?"

I said, "Sure." I did not think much about the request or my response.

She took my draft, walked to the front office, and returned with my English teacher. They both returned to the classroom but were discussing another matter entirely. Mrs. Musumecci gave me back my draft. When she handed it to me, the only thing that came to mind is how my draft probably confirmed why I was assigned to a low-level English class. However, I never questioned Mrs. Musumecci about why she wanted my paper.

Two weeks later, it was the beginning of school day, and I heard my name over the school's intercom. I was asked to report to my counselor's office, Ms. Hooper.

She asked me to sit down and said, "You have a new schedule."

I asked, "Why the schedule change?"

Ms. Hooper said, "It's for your own good."

I took the slip of paper from Ms. Hooper's hand that had my new schedule. My first class was an English class with Mr. Musumecci. I was surprised to read her name on the slip. Nevertheless, I hurried to class given it was fifteen minutes after the final school bell. I walked into her class. Mrs. Musumecci waved me to the front of the class, introduced me to the class, and told me where to sit. I sat down and looked at all the new faces but had no clue what kind of English class was commanding my schedule.

Mrs. Musumecci asked for everyone's attention and said, "Welcome back to Honors English."

I was in Honors English! I cannot fully describe my immediate response as it was filled with mixed emotion. I do remember feeling immediately hopeful about my potential and seriously doubted the validity of assessment outcomes. Mrs. Musumecci never explained what inspired her to take an interest in me or have me in her class. I never thought to approach Mrs. Musumecci to seek understanding about her decision either. I thanked Mrs. Musumecci by doing my best to complete my written work early, read all assigned reading, and participated during class discussion.

To this day, I have no idea what Mrs. Musumecci said or did to get me into her class. However, I will always be grateful that she saw something in me worth taking a chance on. I share this lived experience because one primary goal for becoming a professor was to do what Mrs. Musumecci did for me.

To this day, I utilize my lived experience with Mrs. Musumecci as a driving force to inform how I can be present for students, staff, and other colleagues. Mrs. Musumecci taught me to courageously question and challenge convention thresholds of success. In my case, Mrs. Musumecci challenged the conventions that measure academic success on my behalf. She challenged not only assessment results but also their interpretation and projection of my potential to be academically successful. As a professor, I am always suspicious and leery that conventions can offer a complete view of one's ability to academically succeed. I carry this experience with me when I mentor first-generation students and first-generation junior faculty.

As an undergraduate attending the University of California, Davis, I participated in Minority Undergraduate Researchers in Letters and Science (MURALS), and my official faculty mentor was Dr. Richard Figueroa. Dr. Figueroa—no relation—was a faculty member in the Division of Education as it was known then. Now it's referred to as the School of Education. The Optimal Learning Environment Project (O.L.E), the project Dr. Figueroa directed, examined the early childhood education experiences of dominant Spanish speakers in public school in California. Principally, he wanted to develop more holistic means of assessing dominant Spanish-speaking students because he noticed they were tracked into special education.

Given my stint in special education, I was more than enthusiastic to serve as an undergraduate research assistant on the O.L.E project. Beyond being trained to record and collect data from the multiple sites around California, this opportunity exposed me to graduate students of color. As a Chicana/o studies major, I looked to Chicana faculty to think about quality research as well as having immediate access to graduate students of color earning doctoral degrees. To this point, Alicia Valero, Adriana Echandia, and Denise Isom (graduate students on the project) brought me closer to the idea that maybe I could earn a doctoral degree. MURALS definitely brokered an impactful research experience that inspired me to pursue graduate school. Working alongside Dr. Figueroa and his graduate students, reading the literature with purpose, and presenting at conferences all to better serve students and families taught me how to connect research and advocacy. Specifically, witnessing how the findings from the O.L.E project were presented and discussed in meetings held at the Department of Education in Sacramento with Dr. Bill Honig, superintendent of public instruction, and Shirley Thornton, deputy superintendent of specialized programs, eventually led to thousands of children transitioning out of special education and into a regular classroom was awe-inspiring.

Mrs. Musumecci and MURALS brokered some thinking early in my life about the way success becomes intentionality framed as an individual experience when in reality success is a socially sponsored and socially mediated experience (Rendon, 2006). These two mentoring experiences formed the bedrock on which I stand as a professor who strives to mirror great mentoring. As a professor who mentors a variety of students, I do my best to generously interject with transparency, challenge the status quo, broker new opportunities, and act on the conviction that academic success is a shared responsibility versus something a student shoulders alone.

Mindfully Guiding Me Toward Success and Sustainability by Mentors and Networks

Not always, but more often than not, I am asked who served on my qualifying exam and dissertation committees by other graduate students or peers who are trying to understand my academic development. With trepidation only because bragging is not in my nature, I state Drs. Eugene Garcia, Pedro Noguera, Anne Haas Dyson, and Michael Omi, along with Aída Hurtado as my outside person. Inevitably it is more common than not that most folks will recognize at least two of these names and give me this curious look as if to say, "What was that like?"

I gently say, "Phenomenal."

Individually and collectively, their expectations were high but nowhere near unreasonable. They exposed and inspired me to read beyond the basic load expected for any graduate student. Writing with a clear purpose and critically thinking beyond knee-jerk response helped me to develop a social justice stance fused with logic. The intentional practice of tirelessly considering the trifecta in my work was the objective: policy, practice, and theory. I excelled in all my courses and in my graduate program overall because the strong base of faculty support was always accessible. Complementing this experience, my advisor, Dr. Eugene Garcia, consummately reinforced the idea of being good colleagues within the graduate group of advisees that were assigned to him. I distinctly remember how he underscored the idea that we need to honor this amazing opportunity of receiving a graduate degree by serving the community as opposed to getting caught up in our egos. He often said this because he wanted to help us understand that sometimes we may not receive the appropriate public recognition, but that does not mean our work is not important to the family and children whose lives live at the center our research projects. I believe it was a way for us to stay focused on what mattered and disentangle it from a mind-set of self-importance. As a result of this strong focus on relationship building, many of us who were his graduate advisees helped one another succeed and continue having familial-like relationships. My experiences as an advisee and doctoral candidate shaped my outlook and practice on how to relate to my peers, set a pace of excellence that reflects my intention and focus, and disengage the ego and work with purpose.

As a first-generation Chicana professor coming into my first academic position, navigating the everyday realities associated in the pursuit of tenure inspired me to find a mentor through the Center for Teaching and Learning. Rosemary Papalewis and Mark Stoner were two faculty mentors who played vital roles during my probationary tenure years. Respectfully, unless someone is specifically familiar with Socractic and critical pedagogical approaches as a form of teaching in the classroom, then my efforts might be undervalued and unnoticed. While I know someone from within my department was also going to conduct a teaching observation, I needed an expert in the scholarship of teaching and learning to also conduct an observation to offer some perspective about my teaching.

Hence, I invited Dr. Papalewis to conduct a separate teaching observation and write a letter explaining my teaching practices. Another mentor, Dr. Stoner, helped me edit and strengthen my faculty professional development plan as well as the required reflection statement. Dr. Stoner was not only a mentor, but a white male ally. Dr. Stoner named male, white privilege and how the tenure process has historically operated differently for white and non-white faculty. Hearing this from Dr. Stoner was a huge relief because it affirmed that tenure unequivocally preferences certain forms of research, teaching, and service but makes no effort to outline its constraints to understand new forms of knowledge in the very guidelines used to evaluate files.

The support beyond allies and mentors on my campus proved critical throughout my probationary and post-tenure reviews. Why? The consistent presence and support of Drs. Caroline Sotelo Turner, Laura Rendon, Eugene Garcia, Francisco Rodriguez, Daniel Solorzano, and Aída Hurtado positioned me to pose numerous questions related not just to aspects of professional development, but also balanced with questions related to personal development and well-being. I wanted to understand how they gained stature in higher education while remaining grounded in who they were as people. These mentors helped me to contemplate perspectives and possible practices on how to navigate the social politics of higher education within and outside my campus that fostered a sense of confidence and agency in me. They graciously reassured me when I found myself unsure about next steps in pursuing tenure, offered an extended view on how to keep my research agenda vibrant, and sent positive messages regarding my publications or conference presentations.

Let me state the obvious: these scholars have stature and prominence in the field of higher education so they are not obligated to check on me. But the fact that they choose to set time aside to check on me, to ask me how things are progressing, and to want to be involved in my careers is astounding. I am constantly grateful for their attention and support. Just as their intellectual work fundamentally speaks to social justice, their actions demonstrate a commitment to ensure a next generation of scholars. Not only are these scholars setting a standard of excellence in terms of research, teaching, and service, their mentoring and support of up-and-coming faculty is something that makes me tremendously grateful. Needless to say, I hold sacred the ongoing conversations with these mentors and now colleagues/friends.

When we think of tenure, very little discussion around the role of staff play happens. In my case, staff played a vital role in having a successful file. While I had a mind-set and practice to translate tenure guidelines, the practical steps of putting the file together successfully were the result of sitting down with our administrative support coordinator, Ms. Anne Thomas. Ms. Thomas always attended the Academic, Retention, Tenure, and Promotion (ARTP) workshops to understand the changing policies and practices. Additionally, Sacramento State University was her fourth university and extensively familiar with the demands and expectations with regards to tenure.

While faculty were helpful in terms of having me consider professional development decisions and providing mentoring advice, faculty could not tell me how to best feature my work in the physical binder to be reviewed. Thankfully, Ms. Thomas sat next to me during each probationary year and post-tenure reviews to make sure my file in terms of its index (where you list your evidence) and the accompanying evidence strongly complemented each other. Ms. Thomas made time in her busy schedule to sit with me to make sure my file was substantively strong and polished in appearance. My file was so stellar that after my first year review, the dean of my college asked for it to be used as a model for other faculty. I only mention this not to be self-congratulatory, but more so to make the point the striving for excellence for our Chicana/o and Latina/o community often exceeds what is minimally expected. Reaching beyond mediocrity gives us greater ownership over our tenure reviews. Often times we think other senior faculty will guide us through the process, but just remember to ask staff. Keep in mind that sometimes senior faculty are unavailable or have not attended the most current workshops on tenure like staff. In addition, staff are not required to sit with you, but if they do, remember to thank them as their help contributed toward attaining a lifetime contract.

Becoming a professor meant never working in isolation and really developing a supportive network of folks within and beyond the campus. To supplement the faculty mentoring I was receiving within California, I understood longevity and productivity requires access to a vibrant, intellectual community. The strong desire to understand the national conversations specifically related to the academic success of Latinas/os in higher education inspired me to seek out a higher education network, which is now known as the American Association of Hispanics in Higher Education (AAHHE). According to their website, AAHHE is an agent of change for improving education, thus enabling Hispanic students to fully participate in a diverse society. AAHHE works collaboratively with all sectors of education, business, industry, as well as community and professional organizations to enhance the educational aspirations and to meet the needs of a significantly increasing Hispanic population.

In 2007, I applied and was selected as a faculty fellow by AAHHE. Becoming an AAHHE faculty fellow secured the opportunity to remain consistently productive in scholarship by effectively brokering access to a mentor(s) and networks—to dialogue about issues regarding access and success, racial inequality, and hostile climates as well as the creation of responsive policies and practices—at state and national levels, thus enriching the framing and relevance of my work. As an AAHHE faculty fellow, I received the proper guidance to understand in explicit language and practice the quality of work that needed to be produced in order to experience prosperity as a scholar while at the same time inspire strong of letters in support for my tenure. Understanding how to balance professional and personal commitments to maintain a realistic and reasonable pace and progress for my work while demonstrating productivity, I found extremely helpful from my assigned mentor, Dr. Alberta Gloria.

Prior to meeting with Dr. Gloria, I was expected to share a draft of a manuscript that was intended for publication. This setup would frame my mentoring session with Dr. Gloria. When I finally met with Dr. Gloria, she identified what she liked about the drafted article and where it could be strengthened and finally published. Though receiving constructive positive feedback was familiar to me, for some reason I did not expect such a positive encounter with Dr. Gloria because somehow in my mind it seemed like a prerequisite to know me. Dr. Gloria did not know me, but she believed my ideas and in the drafted manuscript. Sharing my work with someone outside my inner support circle was without a doubt unnerving, but a necessary first step in my professional development.

While I understood that presenting at conferences at state and national levels were meant to broker networking opportunities and expose one's work, there was something quite powerful and distinct having the attention of a senior scholar who didn't know me and validate my work. The continuum of support forming within and beyond California solidified my confidence that tenure review would go smoothly. Rather than feeling isolated, I felt fully supported throughout each tenure review.

Peer support as well as senior faculty mentoring is equally important. My peer support network plays a role in my well-being. I explore ideas about research or writing projects with them, and other times they are the folks I immediately turn to when unanticipated life events happen, like my breast cancer diagnosis in fall 2016. Much like my senior faculty mentors, the friends/colleagues within my peer support network are folks whose work defines a new standard of intellectual excellence and who unapologetically hold onto their values. Prioritizing conferences that enable me to immerse myself in the work and presence of people who are courageous enough to be themselves in the academy, intellectually challenge the status quo, and whose work is meant to make the world a better place are whose sessions I attend faithfully.

In no particular order, my list, though not exhaustive, includes folks like Drs. Aída Hurtado, Laura Rendon, Estela Bensimon, Pedro Noguera, Vicki Ruiz, Michael Omi, Eugene Garcia, Rebeca Burciaga, James Rodriguez, Beatriz Pequera, Yvette Flores, Linda Facio, Enrique Aleman, Danny Martinez, Gloria M. Rodriguez, Patricia Baquedano-Lopez, Jeanett Castellanos, Tara Yosso, Danny Solorzano, Verónica Vélez, Caroline Sotelo Turner, Anthony Rolle, Nancy Acevedo-Gil, Yanira Madrigal-Garcia, Lisceth Brazil-Cruz, Irina Okhremtchouck, Patricia Sanchez, Patricia A. Pérez, Victor Saenz, Luis Ponjuan, Marcos Pizarro, Shaun Harper, Angela Valenzuela, Patricia Quijada, Frances Contreras, Gloria Ladson-Billings, Marcela Cuellar, and Margarita Berta-Avila. I invite the readers to read the work of these people but also make it a point to attend conferences where they are presenting. Introduce yourselves to them. I guarantee you will be transformed and think about academia and the tenure process very differently.

My various experiences with different kinds of support convinced me that existing models of success linked to meritocracy, meaning the individualistic narrative, was completely inaccurate. Mentoring and networks made and continue to make a difference. My public service announcement on mentoring and the importance of networking is channeled through my actions around reciprocity and gratitude.

Sustainability Through Reciprocity and Gratitude

The opportunity to serve others makes my being a professor meaningful. Whether serving as a keynote speaker for a conference; mentoring a junior colleague, undergraduate, or graduate student; hosting office hours for my students; or being asked to serve alongside colleagues to form a panel of experts, these moments are critically important not just because of the utilitarian value of speaking to the tenure criteria such as scholarship and service, but more so because they offer clarity about the kind of service I am providing. Yes, I am sharing my intellectual expertise, but I equally strive to be a visual and audio representation of possibility for the people in the audience who think being a professor is beyond their reach. Let me say, I am not an ego-driven person. I am a values-driven person. By values-driven, I am always striving to keep the bigger picture front and center when I have access to a public platform.

In fact, when I was selected as an AAHHE faculty fellow, I was all too eager to mentor a group of assigned graduate students as well as conduct a professional development workshop for the entire graduate fellow cohort. Nationally, there is not another organization like AAHHE that specifically offers Latino graduate and junior faculty this kind of systemic mentoring structure that focuses entirely on one's success. Toward the end of my associate professor cycle and even after receiving my last promotion to professor, I agreed to mentor junior faculty to continue the mentoring pipeline in AAHHE. In terms of junior faculty, I think it is imperative for senior faculty to support junior faculty as well as graduate students at their respective institutions.

Keeping the continuum of support accessible and available, mentoring locally was important to me. Aside from serving as a faculty mentor with the McNair Scholars Program, Dr. Gloria M. Rodriguez, an associate professor in the School of Education at the University of California, Davis, invited me to mentor doctoral students of color. Inspired by the mentoring structure designed by Dr. Danny Solorzano at UCLA, Dr. Rodriguez adapted a course intended to make sure that doctoral students received the necessary support to thrive in the graduate program. Over the course of twelve years, I co-mentored fifteen graduate students from the time they began until they graduated. We discussed not only the profession, but were all too happy to read position papers, qualifying exams, conference proposals, and debrief conferences and even presented at a few conferences together. For me, this kind of local service combined with the mentoring I have done through AAHHE aligns with meeting predetermined tenure criteria and upholding my values around investing in community.

Conclusion: A Critical Conversation

As a first-generation Latina professor, I strongly encourage you to avoid isolation throughout your continued promotion. Our greatest resource is time, so use it wisely to live in hope and possibility rather than fear or worry, especially when it comes to tenure. My hope is that for the readers of this book, you find the kind of mentors and networks that not only help you advance your research, teaching, and service as a necessity, but also nurture and sustain your humanity and humor and offer you a sense of compassion when situations are not always bright. Or they can provide the kind of wisdom that reignites hope and possibility. I also want you to intentionally access lived experiences that evidence affirmation, belief, and care. Oftentimes academia can be dehumanizing.

So sustaining our humanity is essential aside from polishing our intellect. I always say that if becoming a professor were so easy, there would be more of us. The experiences shared are meant to affirm that showing up for someone can change a person's life. My lived experiences amplified my view of success and underscore the idea that because you had assistance to succeed, that does not diminish the level of commitment and dedication employed to lead the experience.

Until the time comes when there are more Latina professors, I want to share a list that Gloria M. and I spontaneously started typing, given we knew our pathway to tenure was going to be distinctly from our white counterparts. Senior scholars and the literature affirmed that the tenure process lacked objectivity, especially for people of color who were also interdisciplinary scholars (Matthew, 2016; Turner and Myers, 2000). To gain clarity about who we were in the process of attaining tenure, we created the list that was never too far from tapping into the humor, the reality, and the courage it takes to begin the tenure journey. Once we were done writing the list, we realized it was actually helpful, cathartic, and empowering to engage in this process. I hope the list does the same for you. Please remember to hang on to who you are and all that you bring.

Guiding Principles to Achieve Tenure

Drs. Gloria M. Rodriguez and Julie López Figueroa (March 6, 2012)

1. **Remember that your health and well-being are always more important than meeting your colleagues' needs.** Pushing you is their job; pushing back is your job. It's the nature of negotiating. Too often women do not like negotiating. Self-advocacy is never easy, but critical.
2. Learn to say no to set yourself up for success. Just say no and mean it. Say no because doing your job with integrity is important; being focused on your commitment is important. And also reflect that you're being responsible.

3. Even your most trusted colleague's crisis is not automatically your crisis.
4. Co-editing a book prior to tenure can be a kiss of death. Run like the wind no matter how tempting the book title.
5. No matter what the standard for publishing, double it . . . not only because you are a Chicana (i.e., held to a different standard) but also you want to stay marketable.
6. Your students need to want their degrees half as much as you want it for them.
7. Set up healthy boundaries as to when you will respond to emails and calls for students and faculty. You are not an on-call doctor.
8. **Remember that your health and well-being are always more important than meeting your colleagues' needs.**
9. Commit time to network to avoid being isolated in your department and to amplify your resources and opportunities.
10. Good research should not come at the expense of teaching. Good research is partly a foundation for excellence in teaching.
11. Remember to create a reasonable volume of assignments that scaffold meaningful learning as opposed to equating rigor with too many assignments.
12. Remember to take time to have lunch and leave your office for a short walk.
13. Find your best writing hours and hold them sacred.
14. **Remember that your health and well-being are always more important than meeting your colleagues' needs.**
15. To the degree possible, align your service, teaching, and research so you approach tenure in a way that reflects your growth as a colleague, teacher, and researcher. Do not say yes to everything, but be selective. Being selective is your primary responsibility.
16. Do not take anything personal: folks are always trying to get their needs met, even those who claim to be your best allies. This does not mean you need to be paranoid, but just because you're paranoid does not mean no one is after you. (We know this idea is not new, but we could not remember who made this statement previously.) Okay! Be aware, but not expend too much energy being suspicious.
17. Remember, your work matters, and this list is meant to remind you that your talents need to be respected and developed and public. Word! If you agree, say "Yup! Yup!" Can we hear a "Yup! Yup"? That's right. We took it there!
18. **Remember that your health and well-being are always more important than meeting your colleagues' needs.**
19. In the process of achieving tenure, do not overplan. Build flexibility into your schedule for unexpected opportunities and/or life's curve balls. Time is the ultimate resource. A *chancla* well-thrown is the penultimate resource.

20. Keep networking around your writing, research, and teaching. Seek out a resource center on teaching for faculty at your campus; be aware of travel funds and grant opportunities within and beyond your department and college. Remain visible at the local, state, and national levels. Scaffolding is the key.
21. Keep track of all your activities. Create four folders—one reflecting each of the areas identified for tenure (community, institution, teaching, and scholarship). Please check your tenure requirements.
22. Learn to accept and embrace your strengths and excellence when people recognize the power of your work. Even if it is difficult for you at first, practice. It's not about ego but appreciating what you bring.
23. Warning your colleagues may espouse the list above as being important but infringe on your time anyway. Still say no or *no gracias*. Remember they're just trying to get their own needs met. Whatever it takes. It's hard, but do not be scared. It's much more difficult to move from saying yes to no than saying no to saying yes, when possible.
24. **Remember that your health and well-being are always more important than meeting your colleagues' needs.**

The day I received my letter of promotion to professor, I silently read the letter while my eyes welled up with tears of joy. Once I completed reading the letter, I drafted an email to thank all the people who helped me to grow, supported me, and encouraged me to become a first-generation college professor. I often say pursuing a doctoral degree takes courage, but it is not impossible. Three people definitely deserve one final thanks for helping me to develop into becoming someone who is led by values and not ego. First, I want to thank my parents, Macedonio and Maria Figueroa, for being the first teachers to exemplify where courage can take you if we lead with hope, not fear, and live through your values versus ego. In fact, I do not think my parents will ever truly grasp the profound difference they made and continue to make in my life. Secondly, I want to thank Dr. Elisa Facio, my first Chicana/o Studies professor at UC Davis. She was the first faculty member that discussed my potential to do well in graduate school. She recognized something in me, and I decided to trust our conversations that endured across time and space. Not long after beginning my faculty position at Sacramento State, Dr. Facio was home in Sacramento visiting her family, and our worlds aligned, which meant we met up at her family home. There, in front of her parents, I properly thanked her and full expressed my gratitude for being such a great mentor. While I was heartbroken to know of her recent passing on August 30, 2018, I was comforted that I had the opportunity to personally thank her and she was able to witness my being a good steward with her encouragement and support.

References

Matthew, P. (2016). *Written/Unwritten: Diversity and the hidden truths of tenure*. Chapel Hill, NC: The University of North Carolina Press.

Rendon, L. (2006). *Reconceptualizing success for underserved students in higher education*. Retrieved from National Postsecondary Education Cooperative and https://nces.ed.gov/NPEC/pdf/resp_Rendon.pdf

Turner, C., and Myers, S. (2000). *Faculty of color in academe: Bittersweet success*. Boston, MA: Allyn and Bacon.

6 M(other)work as Radical Resurgence
Nurturing Survivance for Women of Color Faculty

Verónica N. Vélez and Anna Lees

This chapter highlights the importance of nurturing intergenerational relationships and survivance (Vizenor, 2008) as everyday acts of resurgence (Corntassel, 2012) for two sister scholars of color—Indigenous and Chicana—navigating tenure-track positions in the academy. As sisters and *comadres*,[1] as aspiring critical educators and accidental mentors, we commit to nurturing the future through revolutionary m(other)ing[2] (Gumbs, 2016). We insist that these futures must encompass our own, our communities, and those of future generations as we struggle to align our work as faculty with our ways of being and knowing as women of color in institutions that don't allow for it. We theorize the necessity of *sisterhood* and *m(other)work*[3] as key to confronting the workings of the university in a time of neoliberal rule (Melamed, 2011), where the bodies and labor of women of color faculty are tokenized by recruitment efforts (Turner, 2002) that are fundamentally antithetical to the very projects of redistribution and decolonization we direly seek. Grounded in this ethic, we navigate toward tenure (and beyond), discovering together what it means to work *within* the university but not become *of* the university (Ferguson, 2012).

In this chapter, we theorize from our lived experiences in tenure-track positions while simultaneously speaking back to institutions of higher education that have become adept at using the language of "diversity," "inclusion," and even "social justice" to perpetuate and deepen the status quo. We frame our *testimonio*[4] in three parts: our sisterhood, m(other)work as radical resurgence; and intergenerational dreams of the postcolonial.

(Part 1) Our Sisterhood

Centering Relationship in Our Journey

We begin by situating our context, both institutionally and geographically, to offer an honest insight of our shared journey, one that is still unfolding as we write this chapter. We work at Western Washington

University (WWU), located between Seattle, Washington, and the Canadian border. WWU defines itself as a regional state institution of higher education that serves approximately 15,000 students, the majority undergraduates, across 160 academic programs.[5] Both of us are housed in the Woodring College of Education, the founding college of the university.[6] Though similar in most ways to other U.S. state-funded, settler-serving colleges and universities, WWU benefits from a strong faculty union that has intervened on several occasions to support us toward tenure and made faculty life, at least for us, more tenable.

We both left our homes in California and Michigan to pursue tenure-track positions at WWU. Like many on the job market post-PhD, options for tenure-track positions are scarce, often requiring a willingness to move far from familiar places and loved ones if we are so lucky to land such a role, particularly in a time when tenure-track positions are being reconfigured for cheaper, adjunct positions in higher education (Jaschik, 2017). We initially met through the mentoring of shared students and efforts to link programming in the college with explicit commitments to social justice. But the forging of our relationship occurred during fall 2015 in a moment of crisis as death threats were launched against two of our students, both women of color (Svrluga, 2015; Relyea, 2015).

This meeting, in a moment of crisis, was a snapshot into the everyday experiences of faculty and students of color at settler-serving campuses in the U.S. (Matthew, 2016). WWU specifically has a history of local attacks by white supremacist-organized groups (Baxter, 2016; Leone, 2014), though not unlike the reality faced by many educational institutions across the country. The instance of violence and activism that ensued in fall 2015 placed the students and us, their mentors, in an increasingly strained relationship to the university administration. This process quickly grew complex as the administration claimed the very terms of "diversity" and "social justice," while concurrently punishing and criminalizing students and faculty at the forefront of these protests. As these protests grew more powerful, institutional responses increasingly sought to co-opt these energies to present the university as a space of open, multicultural dialogue, while in fact it grew increasingly violent.

In the aftermath, administration requested the presence of our bodies to uphold their perceived commitments toward equity. They invited us to participate in forums and dialogues and to lead other conversations across campus about white supremacy and "civil" responses to the hate. They particularly called on us to front relationship building with Indigenous and Latinx/Chicanx[7] communities on and off campus. In these situations, it became clear that our actual ancestry was what they desired, not our scholarly expertise in Indigenous and Latinx/Chicanx studies and other radical traditions. Thus, while our bodies were desired, we were simultaneously rejected as we made evident how settler colonialism and the institutionalization of white supremacy had positioned revolution(arie)s as both the subjects and objects of violence in a variety of sites, including higher education. Our work became viewed by administration as incongruent with institutional goals. As our bodies were co-opted in these spaces and pressure to control our performance grew, our rejection of their desires became increasingly apparent, and our resistance to engage expanded. We made our politics and commitments visible, which led to being labeled as "aggressive" and "uncollegial." We talked together about our shared experiences with faculty meetings and equity committees and found ourselves at a loss for how to behave "professionally" with the smiling faces of colleagues actively engaging in racist and sexist acts (Diggs, Garrison-Wade, Estrada, and Galindo, 2009). We sometimes felt surprised that our basic ways of being in the world were viewed as radical, and we worked to preserve every ounce of who we were in resistance to the neoliberal niceties within which we existed.

As we reflect back on an incredibly violent and frightening experience that solidified our relationship as sisters, we are conscious of our desire to come together and build networks of solidarity apart from crisis interventions. Instead we dream of a postcolonial[8] future where our sisterhood could forge and thrive. We also reflect on our experience as women of color faculty who live away from our lands, families, and communities. The pattern of leaving home to accept a tenure-track faculty line has become the norm in academia. Grounded in Chicana feminist and indigenous epistemologies, we believe our work is conceived within our bodies and ancestry, and as such, relationships in family and community are essential to our professional purpose in ways that feel legitimate and connected to our every day. To exist in the academy and stay true to our aspirations of improving the current experiences of children and youth and foster positive futures for our communities, we must find connections to the space and place we currently inhabit and build family together—with each other, our students, and our extended communities.

Our journey together has led us to theorize our experiences as Indigenous and Chicana faculty who attempt to negotiate our positionalities within academe and our commitments in service to our communities. Building on Simpson's (2017) work, we struggle each day to use the "conventions of the academy to critique settler colonialism and advance our own liberation . . . and continue to produce knowledge and theory in opposition to the academy as resistance, resurgence, and sustenance through our own systems of knowledge" (p. 31). These knowledges—our knowledges—have never been accepted into academic spaces as valid theories or methods. They remain on the outskirts of higher education (and all public education), sprinkled into mission statements and strategic plans to acquire funding and resources, particularly in efforts to seize land (la paperson, 2017).

In a time when the same institutional structures that are harming us as racially and sexually marginalized scholars are the ones that our communities are contesting as they struggle for their own lives. *What is the relationship with each other, our communities, and the institution as we navigate the tenure process? How can our colleagues measure the worth of our work when the very notion of our frameworks is incomprehensible in a colonial context? What does it do to our bodies and our relationships with the earth and the creator to put our ways of being on display for those who have historically and continue to take active efforts of cultural genocide?*

In answering these questions, we also sought to imagine postcolonial futures. Although we had learned the language of the academy and were sure we surpassed tenure expectations, we direly sought frames and theories to ground *for what* and *for whom* we persisted in the work. We write this chapter as one author has recently been granted tenure and the other is preparing her file for review. Our coming together is what made the tenure process livable and possible. We have both put forth at least three times the scholarship and service required at our institution and have outperformed in both quantitative and qualitative teaching evaluations. This over performance was intentional. We were mentored to do double, and we knew what we were up against as women of color employing critical frameworks. It also came with a cost. We do not advocate that this cycle be continued, a cycle riddled with illness and exhaustion. Rather we hope for continued collaboration across our communities to make our work visible and our politics explicit in a way that our very actions against the institutional grain are what protect us the most. As we reflect on our experiences, we recognize our privilege in being able to act transparently within settler-colonial spaces and know that this privilege is a direct result of the efforts and sacrifices made by critical scholars and relatives before us. In dreaming of a future where women of color faculty can work with greater ease, we realized that "in order to participate and demand a society where people help to create each other instead of too often destroying each other, we need to look at the practice of creating, nurturing, affirming, and supporting life that we call mothering" (Gumbs, 2016, p. 9). In our journey toward tenure, *M(other)work as Radical Resurgence* was critical in remaining whole. We explore this in the next section.

(Part 2) M(other)work as Radical Resurgence

Building Our Consciousness as Comadres

In the second part of our story, we share our journey theorizing *M(other) work as Radical Resurgence*. We draw from the work of Gumbs in *Revolutionary Mothering* (2016) and Simpson in *As We Have Always Done*

(2017) to frame our coming to consciousness as m(other)s, or *comadres*, in the academy. For us, becoming *comadres* was a process. As our relationship developed, we also deepened our shared commitments to labor intergenerationally in our service, scholarship, and teaching. This required building a political clarity about our institutional context, whose history and logics are premised on death and destruction (la paperson, 2017). As Simpson (2017) describes in Anishinaabemowin, the word *kwe* means "woman within the spectrum of gender . . . Kwe is not commodity. Kwe is not capital. Kwe does not conform to the rigidity of the gender binary" (p. 29). Simpson (2017) goes on to state that "Kwe as method is about refusal. It is about refusing colonial domination, refusing heteropatriarchy, and refusing to be tamed by whiteness of the academy" (p. 33). As women of color faculty struggling to make sense of our positionality within the academy, Simpson's theorizing of kwe as a method of refusal offers us a foundation to conceptualize our own relationship and our relationships with our students, families, and communities across varying spaces. In our time together, often during our hour-long commute to campus, we dream of the changes we desire in our work. We share stories of our families, our ancestors, and the lands and waters we call home. We share the daily triumphs and failures as well as our constant challenge to find balance within it all. That time together, which we hold so sacred, keeps us alive. Because of this, we feel strong in our work toward *Radical Resurgence* (Simpson, 2017). While we dream of a future we do not yet know (Battiste, 2000), we draw on Simpson's (2017) addition of *radical* to the project of resurgence (Corntassel, 2012; Simpson, 2011). In this, Simpson (2017) defines *radical* as "a thorough and comprehensive reform" (p. 48) and *Radical Resurgence* as "as an extensive, rigorous, and profound reorganization of things" (p. 48). Building on Simpson (2017), we reclaim the word *radical* as we face the plethora of neoliberal academics who learn just enough about justice movements to be dangerous, using such terms as they see fit and thus making necessary our taking back of these terms in order to make clear that our efforts are distinctly different and *radical* in comparison.

As we built our consciousness as *comadres*, we deepened our commitment to the Radical Resurgence Project. Becoming *comadres* signaled our sisterhood and m(other)work coming together. As we journeyed, we theorized *M(other)work as Radical Resurgence* as an effort to (re)claim the "word 'mother' less as a gendered identity and more as a possible action, a technology of transformation [of] those people who do the most mothering labor" (Gumbs, 2016, p. 23). Radically defined, m(other) work insists on nurturing the lives of those who have been deemed disposable, unworthy, and outcast. In higher education, this can take the form of mentoring and advising students experiencing the greatest marginalization and institutional violence, but it can also take the form of m(other)ing knowledge and actions that insist on frameworks that nurture survivance. Though powerfully present in our relationships with our students, we see *M(other)work as Radical Resurgence* as the practice of creating the world we deserve, of valuing ourselves, each other, our communities, and of investing in emerging generations—in *all* aspects of our work as faculty. To name ourselves as m(other)s—as *comadres*—is thus radical. But unlike our colleagues who see radical as "crazy, violent, or from the fringe" (Simpson, 2017, p. 48), we see *Radical Resurgence* as refusing the dispossession of our bodies and lands and working to dismantle colonialism, heteropatriarchy, and white supremacy, along with changes owed to our communities for whom the academy was built to oppress (Simpson, 2017).

These efforts are centered in all aspects of our work as faculty: they drive our research, teaching, and service. In fact, they make possible what has always been siloed conditions of the professoriate to take shape as a holistic experience congruent with our identities and discussed in detail below. This is how m(other)work and kwe as theory drive our work and our existence in the academy. In the next section, we explore how we endeavored to enact *M(other)work as Radical Resurgence* in our daily life as faculty.

Relationship to the University

Inspired by the work of Michelle Tellez (2016) and other women of color who endured the tenure process, we insist on staying grounded in "work that we are politically, spiritually, and emotionally connected to, work that is accountable to the communities that we represent and are tied to" (Tellez, 2016). As we work toward *M(other)work as Radical Resurgence* in relationship to the university, we have begun reconceptualizing the parameters of scholarship, teaching, and service as *M(other)ing Knowledge, M(other)ing Space/Place* and *M(other)ing Movements*. Admittedly, we are unfinished in this process, and as we write this chapter, we share our work-in-progress toward a more sustainable existence in higher education.

(Re)defining our relationship with the university as faculty began early in our dissertation studies, where we were intentional in centering our ways of being and knowing as driving forces in our research, despite advice and training to do otherwise. Neither of us entered the academy with notions of who we would become as researchers, but rather entered the space seeking who we could become for our communities. This is the theory of *kwe*. There is no other way for us. We knew then, as we know now, that we will always be incomprehensible to the academy. Instead of adapting to institutional expectations and norms, we insisted that our work represent who we are, our communities, and our dreams. Our scholarship, service, and teaching thus are not disconnected from our personal commitments. These commitments have allowed us to engage most days as faculty with love and joy. We have maintained a clearer perspective on our purpose within the academy and the role of the academy within our communities. It is with these understandings that we enact *M(other)work as Radical Resurgence* as we construct knowledge, teach, and conduct service, seizing space within our positions to pillage the institution, thus challenging the "neoliberal, individualistic institution that encourages us to do things alone" (Tellez, 2016). We work in relationship to community/family/land and each other, insisting on our roles as *comadres* in *all* we do and, in the process, making clear to the institution that we will not be divided by their notions of objectivity, meritocracy, and competitiveness. We enact these commitments as we make decisions together about the activities with which we choose to engage. Actions as simple as aligning our proposals for university research funding make collective that which is intended to be solitary. (Such grants at our institution explicitly prohibit collaborative proposals.) Gaining such funding then allows us to collaborate on shared goals over the summer months with resources to do so and doing so together.

Our positionality as *educational* scholars is also worth noting. Our research projects are designed to identify educational interventions that are directly linked to improving people's lives, particularly those of children and youth. This context lends itself to interweaving our teaching and service obligations with our scholarship, fashioning the holistic experience that we desire. Thus, m(other)ing knowledge is research, which is service, which is teaching, and the cycle continues. We recognize that the notion of bridging theory to practice is by no means new in the field of education, yet we long for the day when we no longer need to make clear that our scholarship is inseparable from our service and teaching. Preparing our tenure files has painfully demonstrated just how disconnected our work is viewed and assessed by our departmental colleagues. We believe that *M(other)work as Radical Resurgence* has the potential to align our requirements as faculty with our requirements as members of our communities.

By engaging collectively in shared knowledge creation that is situated in anti-colonial practices in service to our communities, we resist settler driven curriculum replacement outlined by Tuck and Gaztambide-Fernández (2013), where "[i]n the context of the academy's competitive individualism, in which there is only one expert in a subject, or only one chapter about a subject is needed in a volume or conference session, the bodies and works by scholars of color are frequently replaced by bodies and works of white scholars" (p. 83). Stated differently, white-stream scholars adopt critical, decolonizing, and multicultural frameworks and then assert a greater expertise of these knowledge than their faculty-of-color counterparts to the detriment of the latter. Our public sisterhood in the college ensures our futurities as Indigenous and Chicana faculty as we situate ourselves strategically on hiring committees, for example, wherein we insist that a single expert in critical and decolonizing theories is not enough, stress that one woman of color in each department is inadequate, and demand that our hiring practices reflect the equity-minded and socially just frameworks that our colleagues *surely* share.

Enacting in the Everyday

In the following sections, we depict how *M(other)work as Radical Resurgence* is enacted through each of the three parameters of our tenure review—scholarship, teaching, and service. We reframe these as *M(other)ing Knowledge*, *M(other)ing Space/Place*, and *M(other)ing Movements*. In each of the subsections, we offer a concrete example of how we have sanctioned these aspects of our faculty responsibilities to both meet the requirements toward tenure and promotion and resist the neoliberal agenda of the institution. We depict how each of the three areas are intentionally interrelated and overlapping. We also highlight how we shared out our work in ways that are both legible and illegible to our colleagues toward tenure, while also preserving the sacredness and integrity of work for and with communities. It is important to note that our path to balance these parameters was not perfect. In fact, much of it is still unfolding. But we have found joy centering *M(other)work as Radical Resurgence* in our life as women of color faculty working toward postcolonial futures. Although still a work in progress, we hope the lessons we have learned offer humble possibilities for others to pursue livability on similar journeys.

M(other)ing Knowledge

The example below depicts a particular project that one of us engaged in with an Indigenous education program. It offers insight of our efforts to engage productively in scholarship while preserving our commitment to community-based research that was not necessarily intended to be shared broadly with the institution. This example also demonstrates ways in which we work to blend the boundaries between research and service that aligns with our ways of being in community.

Washington State has required the teaching of tribal culture, history, and government in all public schools and teacher education programs. This mandate has made work as an indigenous education researcher abundant and necessary. It has also placed our teacher education program and wider university in a position where they must take notice of their relationship with neighboring tribal nations, treaties, and emerging policies. Situated in this context, I have had the opportunity to engage in statewide and local initiatives focused on teacher professional development for indigenous education. One such project, partnered with an indigenous early learning center, I offer quarterly trainings and weekly site visits with classroom teachers. We formed personal relationships, and I actively engaged in classrooms each week with young children to implement a land- and water-based curriculum, addressing the call from the state and greater goals of decolonizing education for indigenous children and families. This work is currently expanding with continued research underway.

However, in my annual reviews I have been intentional in sharing this work primarily as a service obligation with broad connections to my research agenda. I have gained general university funding for a summer project linked to the overarching goals of this work and have not shared details of the partnership at the college level; nor have I requested college support for sustaining the project. The hours I spend with teachers in classrooms each week are the most valuable aspects of my work as faculty. Engaging directly with children and educators around Indigenous curriculum and pedagogy is my dream as a teacher educator, and I have been cautious about sharing those details with an institution that has historically harmed our communities.

Tuck's (2011) rematriation of curriculum studies offers a guide for how I navigate a project that both meets university requirements of scholarship and connects to my particular goals of Indigenous futurities. Tuck's defines rematriation as "the work of community members and scholars in curriculum studies who directly address the complicity of curriculum in the maintenance of settler colonialism" (Tuck and Gaztambide-Fernández, 2013, p. 84). Guided by this framework, I aimed to "(a) repatriate the aims of research/curriculum and (b) use research/curriculum to repatriate knowledge and theories that have been used against us and our interests" (Tuck, 2011, p. 35). I did this by prioritizing the goals of the community, who asked for my involvement. I worked with community leaders to center their tribal cosmologies in the curriculum development, keeping relationships with land and water at the center of our efforts. This was how I *m(other)ed knowledge*. By engaging this research with community and reporting my time spent to the university as service, I was able to both reject institutional ownership of the knowledge we were creating and also protect my time.

Reporting this as a significant service obligation, which it was, allowed me to decline other service work that perhaps would have been disconnected from my core values and goals. It's *that* required service—the endless committees that aim to preserve the colonial structures of higher education—that make us sick. Those are the spaces we have identified as toxic, so we commit to holding onto meaningful scholarship and service with and in our communities (and intentionally blending these boundaries) with all we have.

As we prepared for tenure, we engaged in regular discussions about how we structured our files. We talked explicitly about what should be included and what should be left out—what we would report as scholarship and what would be service. Our decision-making was based on whether we wanted certain parts of our work scrutinized by colleagues who, *at best*, would not understand our work and, *at worst*, would make a case for its lack of "rigor" while asking how they could access our communities for their own projects. It was critical to us that our research agendas be driven by community-identified needs, but we had to be thoughtful about how we included such efforts in our tenure review. It's important to note that we were able to do this because we are not at a research-intensive (R1) institution. We had flexibility to pick and choose what we counted as scholarship to meet the requirements for tenure and had the option to underreport our productivity. This strategic reporting to the review committee allowed us to engage in the work differently, knowing exactly what we were doing to please the reviewers and what we were doing to preserve ourselves, each other, and our communities. This is how we found joy within a painful process and how we engage as researchers that we hope our mentors, our ancestors, and emerging generations can be proud of.

Mothering Space/Place

This example highlights our efforts to redefine our roles in teaching and advising through curricular and programmatic revisions. Again, we share how we disclosed our work and the outcomes of our work in ways that were both legible and illegible. We discuss how we connected our programs explicitly and what aspects of our collaboration remained invisible.

We are situated across two departments in the college of education. One directs the Education and Social Justice (ESJ) program; the other is full-time faculty in the Early Childhood Education (ECE) program and has opted in as affiliate faculty in ESJ. The ESJ program enrolls students from across the university, the overwhelming majority of which are historically underrepresented in higher education—students of color, queer students, undocumented students, and first-generation college students. The ECE program has an explicit commitment to recruiting and retaining students from historically marginalized communities as well and annually enrolls about 50 percent students of color in each admitted cohort. The structure of faculty across departments does not call for collaboration, and in fact, we rarely see many of our colleagues in other departments within the college. However, with the student demographic we serve and as women of color faculty, we often come together in shared advising, which allows us to dream ways in which we could connect our programs intentionally and maintain our values and epistemologies. To do this, we embedded the ESJ minor within the ECE degree program, ensuring that all ECE candidates were eligible to graduate with the minor should they choose to do so. This structure has allowed us to enhance our respective program curricula to overlap with our research and service initiatives (e.g. emphasizing land, water, place, space, community-based organizing, and teaching for social justice). The curricular changes also allowed us to officially connect our advising roles and make the labor of mentoring students across our programs readable in our tenure files.

This connection made clear to our colleagues the extent of time spent serving students who have been historically excluded from higher education; it also made our work advising and mentoring more meaningful. By supporting students collectively, we operated to align with our ways of knowing and being. These intergenerational relationships between teacher as student/student as teacher dismantle the notion of teacher as expert and without relationship. Instead we bring our whole selves into the classroom to support students' holistic needs. Our teaching goes beyond our classroom walls. Our m(other)work goes beyond the classroom walls. And our relationships with students are genuine and grounded in love (hooks, 1994). These relationships are unsanctioned in the university, viewed as *unprofessional*. These same relationships are about survivance in the academy—for students and for us. They are not for or of the institution (Harney and Moten, 2013).

In presenting our files, we were able to depict how we demonstrated collaboration across departments and furthered program curricula in ways that are required of faculty and read well in our evaluations. We were also able to make legible the hours spent advising and mentoring as part of our teaching and service requirements. These clear connections to our faculty roles made this work legible and worthy of promotion. The enactment of collaboration, advising, and mentoring, as well as the overlapping framework of a decolonizing curriculum, were less legible and perhaps incomprehensible to our colleagues. While we received subtle and not so subtle critiques of our students and our relationships with students, there was no platform in our tenure and promotion guidelines for our colleagues to explicitly reprimand or denounce our efforts. By legitimizing the connection of our programs with language from our tenure expectations, we meet faculty expectations while simultaneously working to dismantle institutional structures. We *m(other)ed space/place* within the institution that made our faculty lives possible, providing sanctuary when needed. Again we were strategic about what aspects of our work we shared and what remained invisible, ensuring a successful tenure review while also preserving the intimacy of the relationships that sustained the work.

Mothering Movements

This example offers insight into our decision-making about service. Specifically, we discuss how we made strategic decisions to step down from committees or refuse requests that only sought to engage diversity as performance and did little to further our vision of service. In showcasing this example, we highlight how we relied on each other to negotiate service requests while meeting the requirements for tenure.

It's important to note that much has been documented about the disproportionate amount of service performed by faculty of color (Baez, 2000), mostly women.[9] Although we understood this reality as we entered WWU and its impact on the tenure process, it was difficult to decipher which service commitments reflected a theory of change (Tuck and Yang, 2014) that aligned with our own. Limited knowledge of the institutional context clouded our decision-making about committee requests. As we balanced the tenure demand while knowing that we would be overtapped for service, we relied heavily on our sisterhood to make decisions about service that connected to our teaching and scholarship and drew explicitly on our commitments to community and intergenerational relationships. Our intentionality to *m(other) movements* made clear that our service in the university should allow for radical m(other)ing (Gumbs, 2016), where our efforts could further "an intergenerational movement for collective liberation, in which people of all ages can participate, learn from each other, take care of each other, and dramatically reshape the conditions of their lives." (p. 25).

In line with our vision, one of the most important decisions we made was determining which service requests to *refuse* and committees to *leave*. We realized very early in our positions that university committees with "equity," "diversity," or "social justice" in their title can often work against our understanding of those terms. In fact, they are premised on our dismemberment (Simpson, 2017). We quickly veered from those, citing the overwhelming tax on women of color labor to disappointed colleagues who realized in our refusal they wouldn't make their diversity quota or, even worse, made evident their contradictions of pursuing "diversity" as service for the university. At times the decision to refuse was difficult. Requests often catered to our sensibilities with our students, positioning our decision to say no as a rejection of those we hold most dear in the work. Thus, having each other to reflect became critical. In sharing our struggles to turn down requests, we built political clarity about our service strategies. Over time, we rarely made decisions about what service to engage in without the other's input.

As we dodged particular requests, we also made space for others. We made strategic decisions to join some committees together and collectively support student of color groups and spaces on campus. While we wanted our service labor to be recognized for tenure and promotion, we also sought to be strategic in our legibility about what we were doing. For example, we support and mentor students that are part of community college-to-university program to increase the number of Latinx teachers locally. Many of these students occupy our classes, and we see our daily work with them as part of our commitment to m(other) movements for generations to come, especially given that we were preparing teachers. An addition to this work has been a research component, in which we are exploring the experiences of these students at critical junctures and transitions in their educational journeys. Linking in our scholarship has allowed us to bring our frameworks and epistemologies to bear more directly on the mentoring and programming work of this initiative. At WWU, our "service" for these students was applauded, while we maintained a level of illegibility around the research of these students' experiences. Our intentionality to withhold aspects of our knowledge production around this project aligns again with Tuck's rematrition theories (2011) and is directly connected to our desire to remain distant from the watered-down approach taken by the college around recruitment of students of color that lacks any discussion of retention or resources.

The examples above depict our efforts to (re)imagine required outcomes in research, teaching, and service as tenure-track faculty through a framework that aligns with our commitments and ways of being. *M(other)work as Radical Resurgence* insists that all aspects of our work must be interwoven *relationally*. This means a commitment to each other as sisters and *comadres*, to build with our communities, and to foreground our identities in all aspects of our work. Working within this framework allows us to exist in the academy through a relationship-based ideology, where our productivity as faculty can also refuse the individualistic nature of academe. These examples demonstrate our imperfect efforts at centering relationship in our practice, while also meeting expectations for faculty that are primarily grounded in individual performance measures. We depict how we merged our research, teaching, and service to "confront existing colonial institutions, structures, and policies . . . (as) daily acts of renewal" through everyday acts of resurgence (Corntassel, 2012, p. 89). Our commitment to *M(other)work as Radical Resurgence*, forged in a moment in time where the physical lives of our students were at stake, are essential to our survivance not only as faculty in higher education, but also as members of Indigenous and Chicanx communities within a settler-colonial state.

As we approach the end of our path to secure tenure, we ask, "How do these practices make possible our livability within our work as faculty in ways that we can thrive together?" Knowing that we can't do this alone, we must create the conditions for sisterhood and m(other)work. These efforts and commitments must be intentional and specific. The university will not do this for us.

(Part 3) Intergenerational Dreams of the Postcolonial

A Forthcoming

In this third and final section, we proclaim a forthcoming of what is yet to come. We challenge ourselves to dream the future we do not yet know. We dream structures of education that have overcome Western constructs of age segregation (Bang, Faber, Gurneau, Marin, and Soto, 2016) and human supremacy (Bang, 2015), education grounded in relationships with each other and the lands and waters. We are not yet sure how institutions of higher education fit into this future, but we know that education of the future will be recognizable to our ancestors as they send forth the next generation of scholars who are situated in a society that embraces epistemological diversity. We feel obliged to the Radical Resurgence Project (Simpson, 2017) to ensure that generations to come will thrive and that our work today is work that our ancestors can be proud of while not abandoning our joyful existence in the present.

To reach this postcolonial future (Battiste, 2000), we must nurture the everyday acts of resurgence (Corntassel, 2012) in higher education that were described in the previous sections. By supporting *M(other) work as Radical Resurgence* today, we nurture the survivance of Chicana, Indigenous, and other women of color faculty in higher education. More importantly, we work to secure Indigenous futurities and interrupt settler efforts of replacement (Tuck and Gaztambide-Fernandez, 2013). Although we secured our place as women of color-tenured faculty in a school of education, we are still learning each day what that means and what was lost in the process. We are certain that this institution, whose expectations of scholarship, teaching, and service we have surpassed, will never love us. We are certain that this institution will never understand that this work is conceived and employed within our bodies and relationships (Simpson, 2017). We are certain that while we have learned the language of the academy, the academy will never understand ours. But we remain committed—for us, for our communities, and for future generations.

Notes

1 We use the term *comadre* similar to how Aurora Chang uses it to define her relationship with women colleagues as part of a research and writing collective (Martinez, Alsandor, Cortez, Welton, and Chang, 2015). She defines *comadres* "as those sister friends whom with you share *confianza* (trust). They are non-blood family who have your back every step of the way. They share, listen, gossip, cry, laugh, fall apart and come together at life's cruxes. Perhaps, most importantly they embody a sort of joy that can only be had by friendship bound by a common goal, mutual suffering and a collective sense of goodness" (Martinez et al., 2015, p. 85). We extend this definition to embrace the term's quotidian use in many Latinx communities, whereby *comadre* signifies the shared act of co-m(other)ing and references, more specifically, the m(other)ing of other's people children. Similarly, and as we point out later, becoming *comadres* reflected a process for us of shared labor in which our intergenerational efforts to m(other) knowledge, to m(other) space and place, and to m(other) movements as faculty became core to our survivance in the academy.

2 We intentionally use parentheses to isolate the "other" in m(other), m(other)ing, and m(other)work throughout this manuscript because, like Gumbs (2016), we believe "[t]he radical potential of the word 'mother' comes after the 'm.' It is the space that 'other' takes in our mouths when we say it. We are something else. We know it from how fearfully institutions wield social norms and try to shut us down. We know it from how we are transforming the planet with our every messy step toward making life possible" (p. 21).
3 We want to acknowledge and honor the work of the Chicana M(other)work Collective (www.chicanamotherwork.com) who, among other inspirations and guidance, have pushed us to consider "mother*work*" over "mother*hood*" to foreground the everyday labor of mothering, particularly for mothers of color.
4 Rooted in oral history and human rights struggles, *testimonio* is purposeful storytelling that exposes and disrupts histories that are otherwise subsumed (Cruz, 2012).
5 See www.wwu.edu/about/ for the Western Washington University main website.
6 See https://wce.wwu.edu/history for the Woodring College of Education main website.
7 We acknowledge that this article comes at a time when the label "Latino" and "Chicano" is being challenged to better reflect intersectional identities, particularly gender fluid and gender nonconforming individuals. We have seen various iterations of the term, including (but not limited to) Latinx/Chicanx and Latinx/Chicanx/a/o. We recognize and applaud these efforts, often engaging in conversations with our students about the meaning of rejecting grammatical norms as we seek social justice. Conversations in our classrooms have also revealed the concern that the evolution of labels can often be taken up uncritically, noting that symbols and rhetoric are often the first to be co-opted in struggles for inclusivity. We find ourselves in the midst of these debates and recognize the need to (re)imagine our language to reflect intersectional experiences. Yet we also want to make sure we do so in a way that centers those that will be most affected by the change in representative labels. We have decided to use Latinx and Chicanx here but do so cautiously as we continue to wrestle with how best to represent the complexity of experiences within our communities.
8 We define the term postcolonial not as a period of time, but rather "an aspiration, a hope, not yet achieved" (Battiste, 2004, p. 1).
9 See www.theatlantic.com/education/archive/2016/11/what-is-faculty-diversity-worth-to-a-university/508334.

References

Bang, M. (2015). Culture, learning, and development and the natural world: The influences of situative perspectives. *Educational Psychologist*, *50*(3), 220–233.

Bang, M., Faber, L., Gurneau, J., Marin, A., and Soto, C. (2016). Community-based design research: Learning across generations and strategic transformations of institutional relations toward axiological innovations. *Mind, Culture, and Activity*, *23*(1), 28–41.

Baez, B. (2000). Race-related service and faculty of color: Conceptualizing critical agency in academe. *Higher Education*, *39*(3), 363–391.

Battiste, M. A. (2000). *Reclaiming indigenous voice and vision*. Vancouver: UBC Press.

Battiste, M. A. (2004, May 29). *Animating sites of postcolonial education: Indigenous knowledge and the humanities*. CSSE Plenary Address. Winnipeg Manitoba. Retrieved from http://citeseerx.ist.psu.edu/viewdoc/download?doi=10.1.1.488.6642&rep=rep1&type=pdf

Baxter, E. (2016, June 2). Anti-Semitic incidents on campus revealed. *The Western Front*. Retrieved from www.westernfrontonline.com/2016/06/02/anti-semitic-incidents-on-campus-revealed/

Corntassel, J. (2012). *Everyday acts of resurgence: People, places, practices*. Olympia, WA: Daykeeper Press.

Cruz, C. (2012). Making curriculum from scratch: "Testimonio" in an urban classroom. *Equity & Excellence in Education, 45*(3), 460–471.

Diggs, G. A., Garrison-Wade, D. F., Estrada, D., and Galindo, R. (2009). Smiling faces and colored spaces: The experiences of faculty of color pursing tenure in the academy. *The Urban Review, 41*(4), 312.

Ferguson, R. A. (2012). *The reorder of things: The university and its pedagogies of minority difference*. Minneapolis, MN: University of Minnesota Press.

Gumbs, A. P. (2016). M/other ourselves: A black queer feminist genealogy for radical mothering. In A. P. Gumbs, C. Martens, and M. Williams (Eds.), *Revolutionary mothering: Love on the front lines* (pp. 19–31). Oakland, CA: PM Press.

Harney, S. M., and Moten, F. (2013). *The undercommons: Fugitive planning and black study*. Oakland, CA: Minor Compositions/AK Press.

hooks, b. (1994). *Teaching to transgress*. New York, NY: Routledge.

Jaschik, S. (2017, January 5). When colleges rely on adjuncts, where does the money go? *Inside Higher Education*. Retrieved from www.insidehighered.com/news/2017/01/05/study-looks-impact-adjunct-hiring-college-spending-patterns

la paperson. (2017). *A third university is possible*. Minneapolis, MN: University of Minnesota Press.

Leone, H. (2014, April 24). Western Washington University: The surprising new right-wing target. *Crosscut*. Retrieved from https://crosscut.com/2014/04/wwu-seeks-campus-diversity-amid-presidential-backl

Martinez, M., Alsandor, D., Cortez, L., Welton, A., and Chang, A. (2015). Reflective testimonios of female scholars of color in a research and writing collective. *Reflective Practice, 16*(1), 85–95.

Matthew, P. (2016, November 23). What is faculty diversity worth to a university? *The Atlantic*. Retrieved from www.theatlantic.com/education/archive/2016/11/what-is-faculty-diversity-worth-to-a-university/508334/

Melamed, J. (2011). *Represent and destroy: Rationalizing violence in the new racial capitalism*. Minneapolis, MN: University of Minnesota Press.

Relyea, K. (2015, November 25). Black student criticizes WWU for not taking threat seriously. *The Bellingham Herald*. Retrieved from www.bellinghamherald.com/news/local/article46488630.html

Simpson, L. B. (2011). *Dancing on our turtle's back: Stories of Nishnaabeg recreation, resurgence and a new emergence*. Winnipeg, Canada: Arbeiter Ring Publishing.

Simpson, L. B. (2017). *As we have always done: Indigenous freedom through radical resistance*. Minneapolis, MN: University of Minnesota Press.

Svrluga, S. (2015, November 24). A debate over a mascot, a racially charged threat and another college cancels class. *The Washington Post*. Retrieved from www.washingtonpost.com/news/grade-point/wp/2015/11/24/a-debate-over-a-mascot-sparks-a-racially-charged-threat-and-another-college-cancels-classes/?noredirect=on&utm_term=.599723adf612

Tellez, M. (2016, July 26). Why we must write: A reflection on tenure denial and coloring between the lines. [Web blog comment]. *The Feminist Wire*. Retrieved from www.thefeministwire.com/2016/07/michelle-tellez/

Tuck, E. (2011). Rematriating curriculum studies. *Journal of Curriculum and Pedagogy, 8*(1), 34–37.

Tuck, E., and Gaztambide-Fernández, R. A. (2013). Curriculum, replacement, and settler futurity. *JCT (Online), 29*(1), 72.

Tuck, E., and Yang, K. W. (2014). Unbecoming claims: Pedagogies of refusal in qualitative research. *Qualitative Inquiry, 20*(6), 811–818.

Turner, C. S. V. (2002). Women of color in academe: Living with multiple marginality. *The Journal of Higher Education, 73*(1), 74–93.

Vizenor, G. (Ed.). (2008). *Survivance: Narratives of native presence*. Lincoln, NB: University of Nebraska Press.

7 Triunfos y Tribulaciones/ Triumphs and Challenges

An Intersectional Discussion on Chicana Leadership in the Academy

Marisela R. Chávez, Cristina Herrera, and Patricia A. Pérez

In this chapter, we use an intersectional lens guided by the concepts of *sitios y lenguas* (spaces and languages) (Pérez, 1991) to discuss both triumphs and challenges that we share as tenured Chicana faculty and chairs of ethnic studies departments at public postsecondary institutions in California. We use individual and collective narratives to underscore our journeys as women who identify as Chicana and first-generation faculty who are relatively young in the academy. Our narratives are rooted in Chicana feminist testimonial practices (The Latina Feminist Group, 2001). After sharing our theoretical orientation, we[1] offer introductions and provide a brief narrative of how we arrived to higher education. Based on our collective experiences, we offer small vignettes detailing some of the challenging aspects of our roles and our triumphs, as well as a section outlining how we navigated these roles. Specifically we share the importance of reaching out to Chicana chairs and establishing a "Chicana mastermind" (claiming a space); creating *confianza* (trust) and academic *comadrazgo* (academic kin); and sharing and mentorship. Finally we conclude with practical and policy implications at the institutional and individual levels to support Chicanas and other women of color who are interested in leadership roles.

Sitios y Lenguas: A Chicana Feminist Project

This chapter owes much of its origins to groundbreaking women of color testimonial collections, such as *Telling to Live* and *Presumed Incompetent*, that center the personal experiences of women of color within the academy on which to theorize feminism. Throughout our careers as Chicana academics, but particularly in our current roles as department chairs, what we have experienced within the academy and our respective institutions is inextricable from the realities we face as women of color, whose families and communities are often subjected to intense policing and hostility. As Maylei Blackwell (2003) explains, "Chicana feminism emerged not only out of the gendered contradictions and sexism of the movement but from conflicts with movement discourses that constructed gender norms based on an idealized nationalist recovery of cultural 'tradition' that did not resonate with their lived experience" (p. 66). Blackwell's astute analysis of the origins of Chicana feminism is a reminder, much as the aforementioned collections maintain, that our daily lived realities as Chicanas, women of color, and academics must be front and center as we shape our understanding of the multiple spaces we inhabit. Invoking historian Emma Pérez's (1998) concept of *sitios*, we recognize that claiming a Chicana feminist space of solidarity and support works hand-in-hand with the labor we perform on behalf of our students and disciplines. As "spaces and languages, sites and discourses" (p. 92), *sitios y lenguas* function as "decolonized third world spaces of our own making" (p. 88). The Chicana feminist space we have cultivated simultaneously protects and uplifts us.

Along the same vein, *lengua*, or language/discourse, is also critical to a Chicana feminist project. We use this chapter to offer challenges, achievements, and guidance *in our own words* in a space that was not created with us in mind. As Sonia Saldivar-Hull (2000) highlights, "through their search for a feminist critical discourse that adequately takes into account their position as women under multiple oppressions, Chicana feminists are finding their own organic intellectuals" (p. 46). As Chicana feminists we recognize that discourse is powerful and key to challenging a university system that may consciously and/or unconsciously silence us through omission or blatant disregard as well as exploit us as gendered bodies.

As cisgender, heterosexual Chicanas, we insist on using a theory put into place by a queer Chicana because of our understanding of the centrality of queerness to Chicana feminism. While we recognize the privileges afforded to us as cis-het Chicanas, our many struggles as department chairs underscore the ways in which our bodies, minds, and identities have been socially constructed by dominant culture as dispensable and exploitable (Handler and Hasenfeld, 2007). Before discussing some of these struggles and how we have overcome them, we offer brief introductions of our backgrounds and how we accessed higher education.

Frida S. Badass

My path to higher education is a bit unusual. Growing up I witnessed my aunt and uncle, brother and sister to my mother, work as university professors, so I was always hyper-aware of this career path. However, my parents did not graduate from college, and like many Mexican American/Chicanx[2] families, my larger, extended family was a mixture of college-educated and non-college educated members.

Despite my mother's encouragement that I go to college, graduate school and doctorates were unfamiliar to my mother and family, so I trudged through my doctoral program with little emotional support from other family members. I faced the added challenge of living at home, forcing me to commute long distances while maintaining my family's gendered expectations of contributing to the housework. Research papers and extensive reading assignments meant little to my family. There was still housework to be done. Because of these challenges, I mostly kept to myself, sharing very little of my graduate school life with my mother or brothers, and I quietly did my work while facing racist and sexist microaggressions in the classroom as the only Chicana student in my PhD program. Perhaps the single-most important moment in graduate school came when it was finally time to submit my dissertation proposal. Its importance is due not to the proposal's role in advancing to candidacy, however. At the time, I had little choice but to select one of my professors as an advisor, a white woman and major figure in the field, although my research interests had nothing to do with her area of expertise. So when I submitted my proposal, my professor initially refused to approve it. After exchanging a number of emails with her, she finally called me and told me point-blank, "You can't write your dissertation on women of color, not unless you include Anglo women."

I have little memory of what I said to her after, but after my initial rage and frustration wore off, I sought the advice of a colleague of mine who had been serving as my informal mentor, a wonderful Chicana professor who hired me to teach part-time in her department at a nearby university. She encouraged me to find a Chicana professor at my institution to serve as my dissertation chair, and after a few months, I did. And she eventually guided me and supported me through the completion of the dissertation and the defense.

Valentina S. Poderosa

Growing up, attending (and graduating from) college was a given. My parents, immigrants to the U.S. at a very young age, are both college graduates, as are some of their siblings, though their paths to completing their degrees were circuitous. They both have post-baccalaureate degrees. Due to my parents' careers and social circles, I grew up among other professionals of color and professors, and I spent quite a bit of time on college campuses. By the time I got to college, however, I experienced quite a culture shock. The transition from a large urban high school was rough, but I eventually found my way, both socially and academically. My path to the professoriate emerged due to my participation in an undergraduate summer research program, where I met the professor (at another university) who became my advocate, cheerleader, and mentor.

After college, I taught high school before entering into a master's program. I was fortunate to not have family responsibilities or obligations, and I moved away from home to evaluate whether this was the path I would continue. I discovered that I loved my discipline. Additionally my mentor created a family of graduate students, showing those who had come to study with her that community was essential for thriving in an institution that did not always welcome students such as us. When it was time to apply to doctoral programs, my mentor expertly guided me through the process.

I attended a prestigious doctoral program in my field, with a Chicano advisor, where I was groomed to land a tenure-track position at a research university. Again I was extremely fortunate to enter into a community of mostly women and women of color scholars in my field who served as a source of support, encouragement, and inspiration, especially when the going got tough. They became—and still are—*familia*. We supported each other through explicit and veiled racism and sexism.

One experience stands out. At the point of transition where one advances to candidacy, a professor in the department attempted to block my advancement based on what he perceived as my lack of interest in his particular specialty. I was not alone in this. He attempted the same for another student of color in my cohort. He was not successful because my doctoral advisors lobbied on my behalf, but I remember feeling both fury and fear at the thought of being deemed unsuitable for a degree based on the opinions of one person.

Being married and having a child in graduate school also influenced my experience. On the one hand, having the emotional and financial support of my spouse was extremely important. On the other hand, the kind of time I felt I needed to invest in reading and writing and to succeed put a hamper on my marriage, especially since my spouse was far removed from academia. My daughter was born in the fourth year of my program. During my pregnancy, I did not tell any of my professors, nor my advisor, until it was absolutely necessary.

After my daughter was born, I kept a low profile until she was about five months old and I had to return to campus to fulfill my last obligation as a teaching assistant. Sending my daughter to daycare was a difficult transition, and having a family while being in academia is still a path I negotiate to this day.

Guadalupe B. Chingona

I was fortunate to be one of the few students of color tracked into my public high school's college preparatory track. I pursued college because that is the assumption teachers and counselors made about me as an honors student. In my undergraduate program, a professor in my ethnic studies class remarked that the class was witnessing a future professor as

I gave a presentation. As a first-generation college student, that option had never crossed my mind, but a seed was planted. As I neared my senior year in undergrad, I was still unsure about the career path I wanted to pursue. A wonderful mentor shared, "When in doubt, stay in school." And that is what I did. Eventually my path would lead me to a prestigious and highly ranked doctoral program in the discipline. While the program was preparing students for future faculty positions, I was still not convinced that path was for me. I had very few Chicanx and Latinx faculty to serve as role models. While I had strong examples, the few I had been exposed to did not make the faculty lifestyle appealing. The few Chicana and Latina faculty around me had experienced divorce and bad breakups, and many lived miles away from their families. Few had children.

When I was on the job market and combing through the available opportunities, it was the cultural and ethnic studies faculty positions at public universities that I gravitated toward because the job descriptions most identified with my core values and commitments and seemed to be the best "fit." Based on my limited knowledge, I was not aware until I was well into my doctoral program that I did not have to pursue a faculty position at a research-intensive university. Publish or perish. Publish or perish. Publish or perish. Not exactly an inviting mantra. While students were being trained to pursue faculty positions at such institutions (and you likely did not share if you did not plan to or potentially miss out on fellowship and teaching opportunities), I would find my way to a comprehensive state university that provided a better teaching-research balance. Although a former professor would remark it was a good stepping-stone, in my view it was a chance to work with a student demographic that I identified with as well as continue to pursue the research I loved at a more manageable pace.

Collective Narratives: Challenges to Our Roles as Chairs

Our individual experiences, though unique, bear many similarities, demonstrating the ways in which we face added burdens as women of color. We share our collective stories to situate ourselves within an overall discussion of women of color academics but also as a measure of solidarity with each other as Chicana department chairs within institutions that have not always been supportive, safe spaces for intellectual exchanges.

We have had the privilege of serving as faculty members of ethnic studies departments for over a decade. Ethnic studies departments were born out of struggle, civil rights movements, and student protests, among other forms of resistance, with the common thread of social justice and student empowerment underscoring their creation (Orozco, 1986, 1997). Ironically, and to our surprise, this does not mean that all our colleagues share the same values of fairness, justice, and commitment to civility.

Indeed we have had some of the strongest challenges to our roles as faculty and now chairs from other people and women of color both inside and outside our departments. While there may be an assumption that our values are the same because we are all faculty in ethnic studies and that we "have each other's back," this may not be the case in all circumstances. Whether we are being challenged on a decision because we are women, women of color, or young women of color is difficult to disentangle. However, what we wonder is the extent to which we would be challenged if we were older, white, and male in the same position. In many ways, our identifiers and phenotype encourage more challenges. We are not what a professor "looks like."

When we became department chairs, we were optimistic about the kinds of positive changes we could lead for our departments, especially with regard to making our departments more attractive to students, fostering a collegial and friendly department atmosphere, and implementing needed policies that we believed would improve and clarify internal department processes. We have accomplished many of our goals, which we discuss later, but our achievements have been tempered by the following examples of the challenges we have faced as Chicana chairs. These include but are not limited to:

1. We have been undermined by colleagues who had belittled us in the past, and we have had varying levels of support from the administration.
2. We have been accused by administrators of bias against faculty in our own departments, without evidence.
3. We have been belittled by colleagues and administrators through name-calling, often in public.
4. We have been verbally attacked and threatened by male colleagues for issues such as course schedules.
5. We have been accused of unfair actions when we follow university policy.
6. We have felt fear for our safety and made extra accommodations to never be alone with certain colleagues.
7. Our positions as department chairs have been threatened by disgruntled colleagues.
8. We have been accused of being unprofessional, attempting to undermine other faculty members, and conspiring with students against faculty members.
9. Our attempts at positive change for our departments have been undermined by negative actions on the part of colleagues.
10. Changes to department policy and curriculum revisions have provided opportunities for colleagues to attempt to thwart these changes, at times involving deans and both college and university committee engrossment.

11. We have been left to shoulder tasks and work because colleagues would not take joint responsibility for department needs.

In the following section, we revert to the "I" for purposes of anonymity and confidentiality and offer details of some of the aforementioned examples.

By the end of my first year as chair, I felt like I had survived a war, but it turns out I was far from facing more threats to my position. A former dean of ours accused my colleagues and I of unfairly treating a lecturer in our department, and she threatened me at an end-of-the-year reception, calling me *mijita*[3] and warning me that if I did not treat a lecturer to her standards, she would later come back to my department as my adversary.

When I became chair, I was optimistic, thinking to myself that perhaps I could help usher in a new departmental ambience, going so far as to present my colleagues with our academic policy manual statement on collegial behavior at our first meeting of the academic year. However, within months of my first year, I was undermined by the same colleagues who had belittled me in the past, as they continuously complained to my dean when they were outvoted at departmental meetings. I had several drop-in meetings from my dean, who would talk to me about inclusivity, saying little when I told her that my colleagues' behavior was an attempt to question my legitimacy as chair. That same year, the colleague who had once verbally attacked me threatened me again, this time in my office when he met to speak with me about his upcoming course schedule. He raised his voice, repeated the words, "We'll see what happens," and accused me of deliberately giving him an unfavorable schedule. I had no choice but to speak to my union representative and faculty affairs vice president, and I told them what was true since my first year as a tenure-track faculty member: I did not ever want to be alone with this man because I feared for my safety.

Over the next year, I would attend numerous meetings with our campus human resources, faculty affairs, and union representatives, but this former dean and senior colleagues were not punished for their threats and attempts to sabotage me. I later learned that one of my senior colleagues had met with the former dean to try to remove me from my position based on false accusations against me. The low point came this last fall when, after yet another impromptu meeting with my dean, who more or less told me to "play nice" and do what I was told, I could no longer contain my anger and stress, and I had a full-blown panic attack in my colleague's office when we were supposed to discuss a project. He, along with my two close friends, finally understood the depths of what I was experiencing. Although this was the low point, the first time I had ever visibly melted down on campus, my colleagues proved themselves to be loyal and kind, and I have relied on their help in more ways than one.

I became chair of my department under trying circumstances, after many years of mistrust among faculty members. As chair, I organized a department retreat, something the department had not done for many years. Both full-time and part-time faculty attended the retreat to witness a shouting match between me and another full-time faculty member who accused me and another woman colleague of conspiring against him via our advising of student organizations. That meeting has set the tone for my tenure as chair. In my time as chair (and prior to as well), I have been called unprofessional and undermining and have been accused of conspiring against said faculty member.

In a small department, when one member checks out, the rest, who happen to be women, are left to do the work of the department: meetings, campus committees, curriculum changes, and so forth. It is especially difficult when the faculty member who has checked out only expresses interest and objection after all the work has been done. Recently I took the leadership of revising the department curriculum. It had not been updated in over ten years, and its structure was not working for students or faculty. The other full-time faculty member and I (and some of the part-time faculty members) participated in a process that took over eighteen months, most of which took place during department meetings. When we submitted the proposal to our college committee, after many consultations with various levels of administrators, my colleague wrote a letter of opposition to the college curriculum committee, copying a variety of committee chairs and administrators, objecting to two particular changes. Although the proposal had been in the works for approximately one and a half years, this was the first time my colleague had any input. The college curriculum committee proposed a compromise that would have added units to the major. I objected to the change and asked that the university curriculum committee take the matter instead. I was appalled that the committee would take this objection seriously, especially since it was a member of my own department who had many opportunities to weigh in on the curriculum changes but only chose to do so after the proposal had been submitted. I attended the university curriculum committee meeting when the proposal was on the agenda and explained my objections to the compromise.

I know many ethnic studies departments are not inclined to air internal issues to the larger campus community since our existence seems to be inherently questioned. Internal conflicts only lend credence to the department's liminality. But I decided that when my colleague sent the first complaint, the dirty laundry had already been aired, and I was forthcoming in my descriptions of the process and my objection to a faculty member complaining after the fact when he did not participate whatsoever in the process. In the end, the university curriculum committee approved the curriculum revision with no changes. I share this experience as an example of one of the ways being chair of an ethnic studies department has been challenging. However, it is also an experience where I cultivated support among a variety of constituencies on campus, developed relationships across campus, and worked closely with faculty and administrators to move this along. I also reminded myself that this was for the success of students and not about personal issues between faculty. I also believe it is about what battles to fight. There are many that I believe are not worth my time and energy. This one was.

I write this as chair in a department that has been overwhelmingly male and heteronormative. As a young, tenure-track professor in this same department, I was often referred to as *la niña*[4] because I was the youngest member, a not-so-subtle reminder by the senior Chicano males that I should remember my "place." In my first year as a faculty member, the chair at the time berated me for incorrectly placing a class cancelation notice in my syllabus, something I did not know since nobody ever told me. He slammed the door of my office, pointed his finger in my face, and yelled at me in a way no one had before. At the time, I did not think to tell anyone of his abuse. Who could I talk to? Needless to say, his behavior did not stop, and I, in addition to two other tenure-track colleagues who would eventually become some of my closest friends, would be targets of his rage. Over the next several years, this chair, along with another senior faculty member in the department, who later became department chair, would commit some of the most heinous acts for which they were never punished. For example, when my colleagues and I complained to the senior faculty member about our chair's abuse, the senior colleague told us, "That's just how he is. You need to just accept it."

Triumphs as Department Chairs

While certainly the struggles we face as Chicana chairs are ongoing and challenging, we believe it is equally important to highlight our many triumphs, both collective and individual, that we have achieved amidst these hardships. As chairs of departments that have historically had to justify their existence in neoliberal attacks against higher education, we have successfully overseen departmental growth. In the face of budget constraints and bureaucratic policies, we have had no choice but to be creative with the limited resources available to us. We have guided students to success, mentoring them through the process of applying to graduate school and post-baccalaureate careers. Given that we may be the few Chicana professors with whom our students may come into contact, we are often sought out by students as mentors and role models, which demonstrates that our work exists beyond the confines of the classroom. As Chicana scholar-activists committed to our students, departments, and research, supporting and advocating for our community is part and parcel of what we do every day in our capacity as the visible "faces" of our departments.

For us, the work we do as chairs is grounded in this deep commitment to social justice, and we remain devoted to our values as a guiding principle. This means that we have had to learn to speak out, albeit the hard way, when we have been victims of unfair attacks by fellow colleagues and administrators. Although facing these attacks has tried our patience and sanity, we have stayed the course, becoming resilient in the process. We are all tenured, and two of us have recently earned the rank of professor, remarkable feats. One of us was the first woman to achieve tenure since the department's founding in the late 1960s.

To survive and thrive in our institutions and academia, we have learned new skills along the way, knowledge and strategies for which graduate school offered no preparation. As chairs, we manage the day-to-day running of our departments, lead department meetings, structure course schedules, and assign courses, and we are the first stop when students in any of our department courses have a complaint. We are also frequently in contact with administrators, forcing us to learn strategic and effective communication to advocate on behalf of our departments. Department chairs represent their respective departments, which means that our actions and behaviors are subject to criticism when we act in a way that is deemed too "radical" or "subversive." Thus, our response to unfavorable criticism is equally important. We cannot be too reactive, or we will suffer the consequences. At the same time, we must be savvy and politically wise enough to distinguish between those battles that are worth fighting and which ones are best left alone. For example, we are deeply committed to participating in decisions regarding tenure and promotion of colleagues; fair and transparent resource allocations to our departments; issues such as appropriate enrollment numbers for our department pedagogical practices; and inclusion and equity across our respective campuses. We have learned, however, that our time and energy is not best used by being involved in issues such as internal battles between departments or individual faculty members outside our departments, complaints and protests that take a life of their own via email, or being pulled into university struggles where we see our departments as token representatives.

Being Chicana chairs is a balancing act. Constant demands of our time mean we have to prioritize our own research and scholarly activities, although this is a major challenge. Nevertheless, we have maintained our scholarly agendas, contributing to our respective fields despite our heavy workloads. This has required us to be cognizant of our minds and bodies. We are not interested in free labor and find it easier to say no when we are expected to take on additional labor without compensation.

Our Chicana mastermind is one such way we have sustained and uplifted each other. Forging alliances and critical networks have been key to our well-being. Though we use our monthly chats as a way to share ideas and solutions involving our work, more often than not, we use this coveted time to simply inquire about each other's health and well-being. Although this may seem minor, recognizing each other's humanity is a radical act of Chicana solidarity and love. These monthly chats are prioritized, and we rarely cancel them. We work in a setting, academe, which is not conducive to boundaries and work-life balance, where it is common for academics to work excessively long hours. This is entrenched in academic culture. But as women of color who explicitly know that our communities have been historically exploited through unfair labor practices, we refuse to contribute to academic culture's expectation that we act as machines rather than as flesh-and-blood beings with lives and families. All three of us are married to partners, have children and/or pets, and see our private lives as off-limits for the likes of our institutions. While we are firmly committed and devoted to our careers, we have each achieved remarkable career success without sacrificing our commitment to our families, who sustain and support us within an institutional culture that has not been family-friendly. Indeed this collaborative chapter is a labor of love, an homage to the *comadrazgo* we have cultivated through our Chicana mastermind.

Managing and Navigating Our Leadership Roles

Although the narratives and collective scenarios that we have discussed have caused us undue stress, anger, and frustration, we have also found ways to both manage and navigate our roles successfully as Chicana department chairs. Our methods include claiming and creating a space for ourselves, creating *confianza* and academic *comadrazgo* as well as mutual sharing and mentorship.

Claiming and Creating Space

Our particular experience began via social media when one of us reached out upon hearing that the other two were new chairs of ethnic studies departments as well. We talked via social media and email, and one of us had the idea of establishing a Chicana/Latina mastermind, an idea influenced by the National Center for Faculty Development and Diversity. We want to highlight the importance of reaching out to others who are in the same or similar situation, regardless of geographic location. It is a risk to reach out to people whom you do not know, and it may take trial and error to find the right fit, as it did with our group. Once we met virtually, we realized that our experiences were ridiculously common and repetitive. We often joked that we could trade places and our experiences would be the same. In setting up a group that met monthly due to our schedules, we created a space for ourselves where one did not exist and was not meant for us. We took advantage of social media and technology as well as opportunities to meet in person at a conference. We also utilized instant messenger when we needed more immediate feedback or needed to vent quickly before imploding. These spaces were critical to our collective sanity.

In utilizing the mastermind strategy, the space both emphasizes and reminds us that we are not alone in our journey; it also provides an arena free of prejudice or judgment. Our regular meeting schedule, which we all make time for in the midst of family and professional obligations, provides an opportunity to strategize around issues and problems and check in about work and personal lives. Our mastermind also allows us to recognize that as chairs, we do not have to be superwomen and take the burdens and responsibilities all on our own. The mastermind provides a space where we can be our own cheerleaders and remind ourselves that it is okay to be proud of our achievements as chairs, whether it be getting through a difficult department meeting, handling conflict with administration, or going through more positive situations, like receiving promotions and awards.

Creating *Confianza* and Academic *Comadrazgo*

In establishing our Chicana mastermind and due to our very similar experiences as tenure-track faculty and new department chairs, we were able to establish *confianza*, or trust, quite quickly and easily. Our mastermind became a safe space where we could share without any judgment, especially important given the matters we shared with one another, both professional and personal. Although we were far apart, our *confianza* eventually became an academic *comadrazgo*, an academic kinship or chosen family who understood the trials and tribulations of our faculty, academic, and chair roles. Our academic *comadrazgo* sustained our souls and ourselves when we leaned on each other for support, held each other up when the burdens became heavy, and reinforced that we made difficult decisions because we had the best interest of our students and our department at heart.

The truth is, without allies, we have no idea how we would have survived what we never imagined we would collectively face as chairs: threats, betrayal, varying support from administration, baseless accusations of bias, colleagues who do not share the workload of the department, and continuous attempts to remove us from our positions. While our experiences do not necessarily account for all women of color in similar positions as ours, the constant battles we face are inseparable from the realities of our lives as younger Chicanas who refuse to be silenced. We have no doubt that the threats we have faced are due to the fact that we have used our positions to question unfair practices from our administrations and to call out senior male faculty members in our departments for their unethical and harmful behavior. Speaking out has placed us in the firing line of threats, even coup attempts, revealing the inconvenient truth that a vocal Chicana is a "dangerous" Chicana for the likes of institutions such as ours that do little to protect and nurture women of color in department chair positions.

Sharing and Mentorship

Our Chicana mastermind has also been a space where we practice sharing and mutual mentorship. It is a space where we are not competitive with one another (as academic culture expects us to be). As chairs that go through very similar experiences, we share our resources as a strategy to build each other up as we move forward in our careers. For example, we have shared public documents, templates, and campus practices with one another because our institutions are at different levels of having various policies in place. We have mentored one another regarding shared strategies on how to manage our time more efficiently as well as strategies on how we have successfully handled complex and conflict-laden issues, be it with students, colleagues in our departments, or administration. Our sharing and mutual mentorship has been cathartic because in doing so, we are reimagining the neoliberal university. Our practices have also been therapeutic because we have celebrated life and professional achievements and validated each other's experiences, feelings, and ideas.

We have also recognized the importance of "paying it forward" so we may be helpful to other first-generation faculty and especially women of color faculty. We have also used our experiences to mentor faculty in our respective professional associations and at our own institutions. We have shared our experiences as chairs at the American Association of Hispanics in Higher Education (AAHHE) faculty fellows workshop, and we do so again through this chapter.

Practical and Policy Implications

Based on our collective challenges, triumphs, and experiences as Chicana faculty and chairs in academe, we offer the following policy and practical implications to support future women of color who are interested in serving in chair or administrative roles.

Institutional

Structurally, the U.S. higher education system is set up in a very hierarchical manner that is a manifestation of the patriarchal and individualistic society that we live in. Unfortunately universities were not created with women of color in mind, let alone women in leadership roles. As a result, we need to be proactive about seeking out professional development opportunities that will go beyond the basic "balance a budget" workshop. Resources like the National Center for Faculty Development and

Diversity, which were made with faculty of color in mind, can offer various forms of support and information depending on your career goals. Other programs such as Higher Education Resource Services (HERS), for women only, or the American Council on Education (ACE) Fellows program, not gender exclusive, can provide valuable leadership training, though not specific to women of color. Further, training for new or incoming chairs such as through the Council of Colleges of Arts and Sciences or in the California State University system, the annual system-wide department chair workshop, can be helpful, but we urge you to lobby deans and administrators in your faculty development or academic affairs offices about financially supporting the growth of leadership from within your campus and bringing coaches to work specifically with women of color to cultivate a more diverse and equitable higher education leadership pipeline. If the interest is strong enough, creating small cohorts of new women of color chairs and pairing them with more experienced women of color chairs, if they exist at your campus, would provide an invaluable space for all participating. Support from administration may consist of implementing the structure of the mentorship program, providing space and stipends, as well as funding coffee or lunch for participants on a consistent basis. While we may share similar challenges and experiences with other chairs, as Chicanas and women of color, we confront different struggles that may not be as salient for others.

In addition to cohorts, we suggest the creation of informal or formal mentoring programs designed for women of color faculty members who wish to serve as department chairs and/or other leadership positions. For example, on one of our campuses, there is a faculty and staff mentor program that pairs faculty members with administrators on campus, which fosters relationships between two groups of campus employees to build trust, confidence, and leadership skills. One of us participated in the program and was mentored for one academic year by a campus dean, a male Latino who served as an invaluable ally and a staunch supporter. Meetings were informal, typically intended as time to ask for recommendations and advice on addressing departmental issues in a confidential space. While this mentoring was highly beneficial, we suggest that mentor programs should be created with more intentionality around issues of gender and race so that women of color faculty are mentored with more senior campus officials who recognize the unique struggles we face.

Individual

When you are serving as a chair, it can be an isolating experience. As women of color, that isolation may be and feel especially heightened. To circumvent some of this isolation, we recommend seeking out other chairs or people in similar leadership capacities both within your institution and outside of your home campus. We have learned that those with more experience in leadership capacities will be able to share valuable methods to make the position of chair amenable with a continued research and publication practice. For example, they may be able to provide various ideas for you to negotiate reassigned time for research, especially for those of you who become chairs as associate professors and plan to apply for promotion to full professor. While the more experienced leaders within your college and/or institution can offer knowledge and expectations regarding your campus culture, folks outside your institution can share a different way of approaching your role. With technology, it is much easier to reach out to chairs outside of your local area to share knowledge, commiserate, and strategize about how to address various situations. Virtual meeting spaces and social media platforms allow us the opportunity to connect with one another where otherwise we would not be able to because we live in three different counties in California. Because there are very few Chicanas in this position, these moments and spaces to connect become all that more important and critical to your well-being.

In most cases, the chair role is a limited term wherein you return to your faculty role and the chair responsibilities shift to someone else at the conclusion of your term. During your term, is important not to put your important relationships on hold. Despite the time constraints, you must build time in for your family and loved ones. These relationships should be a priority as they will sustain you during the challenging times in your chair role and will hold you up after the fact. While certainly magnified, challenging experiences and opportunities are not limited to when you are in a leadership role. However, just because you are in a leadership role does not mean you should use that as an excuse to ignore your important relationships. When time is limited, this may look like a coffee date with your partner or a quick phone call with your best friend. Additionally it is critical to make time to decompress. Meditation, naps, pleasure reading, and solo walks outside are all examples of self-care that can remind you what is important and truly valuable. These strategies will help humanize you if you are in a space that is constantly trying to dehumanize you and challenge your value system.

As we shared, reflected, drafted, edited, and shaped this chapter, many of our individual stories turned into collective narratives because we had gone through many of the same experiences as women, Chicanas, and in our capacities as chairs. In many ways it was reassuring and cathartic that we were not alone in these spaces. However, it also signaled the manifestation of a much larger problem in academia and society at large. But this does not have to be the case. We view this chapter as a form of Chicana resistance and challenge to the individualistic, patriarchal, hierarchical, and neoliberal university that does not value us as human beings. We choose to impart our knowledge and share our experiences with the hope that future Chicana and women of color leaders will too find solace within these pages and continue to resist in their own ways.

Notes

1 It is important to note that throughout the chapter we will use the "I" to situate ourselves as individual subjects, but we will use pseudonyms because we are cognizant of the potential for backlash. We also use the collective "we" both as a form of solidarity, to maintain confidentiality, and to bring focus to our shared experiences.
2 The term *Chicanx* or *Latinx* refers to our recognition of diverse gender identities that do not fit within the traditional terms *Chicana* or *Chicano* that position gender along the narrow binary of man/woman.
3 Spanish for "young daughter."
4 Spanish for "little girl."

References

Blackwell, M. (2003). Contested histories: Las hijas de Cuauhtemoc, Chicana feminisms, and print culture in the Chicano movement, 1968–1973. In G. F. Arredondo, P. Zavella, A. Hurtado, N. Klahn, and O. Najera-Ramirez (Eds.), *Chicana feminisms: A critical reader* (pp. 59–89). Durham, NC: Duke University Press.
Handler, J. F., and Hasenfeld, Y. (2007). *Blame welfare: Ignore poverty and inequality*. New York, NY: Cambridge University Press.
Orozco, C. (1986, 1997). Sexism in Chicano studies and the community. In Alma M. García (Ed.), *Chicana feminist thought: The basic historical writings* (pp. 265–270). New York, NY: Routledge.
Pérez, E. (1991). Sexuality and discourse: Notes from a Chicana survivor. In C. Trujillo (Ed.), *Chicana lesbians: The girls our mothers warned us about* (pp. 159–184). Berkeley, CA: Third Woman Press.
Pérez, E. (1998). Irigaray's female symbolic in the making of Chicana lesbian sitios y lenguas (Sites and Discourses). In C. Trujillo (Ed.), *Living Chicana theory* (pp. 87–101). Berkeley, CA: Third Woman Press.
Saldivar-Hull, S. (2000). *Feminism on the border: Chicana gender politics and literature*. Los Angeles, CA: University of California Press.
The Latina Feminist Group. (2001). *Telling to live: Latina feminist testimonios*. Durham, NC: Duke University Press.

8 Latina Administrators Practicing Resonant Leadership in the Borderlands

Patricia Arredondo

> To survive the Borderlands you must live sin fronteras/be a crossroads.
> —Gloria Anzaldúa (1987, pp. 194–195)

Author's Personal Introduction and Asset-Based Approach

In *Mujeres Latinas, Santas y Marquesas* (Arredondo, 2002), I share that my role models were strident *mujeres* (women), my *abuela* (grandmother), my *tía* (aunt), and of course my mother. Their cultural capital was derived from their Mexican *mujerista* (woman) socialization, primarily one of caring, nurturing, spirituality, and putting their families first. From my abuela, I learned about self-determination, entrepreneurship, and strength through spirituality. My tía took a train across the country to protect her eight children from an abusive spouse, worked continuously to ensure their well-being, and became a missionary in the prisons to encourage spirituality. From my mother came encouragement for homework first, reading, being a loyal daughter, and having confusion about ethnic identity. My feminist father also played a central role in my personal and professional development. He looked out for my abuela, my tía, and of course our family of nine, affirming a sense of security and empowerment. From all of these role models, I learned about leadership and how to enact it through integrity, poise, and persistence. As my career in higher education leadership unfolded, I relied on familial examples of self-determination and empowerment as well as an affirmative cultural identity as I negotiated the borderlands and grew in resilience.

My worldview of academic leadership and specifically about Latinas as leaders is informed by my various roles and experiences at predominantly white institutions (PWI) over a twenty-two-year period. Department chair, principal investigator, and co-principal investigator on federal grants, dean, senior vice president for student initiatives, associate vice chancellor for academic affairs, and president of a school of professional psychology are the positions that I held. Generally the staff was predominantly white, but by the time I left a position, the faculty and staff were more visibly diverse. For example, I was dean of the School of Continuing Education, University of Wisconsin-Milwaukee (UWM), for four years. When I left, the staff was 35 percent persons of color, the highest percentage in any UWM school or college. At other institutions, I supported the enrollment of more students of color and the hiring of administrators, faculty, and staff from underrepresented groups. These actions to lead change for inclusion were inspired by other professors of color and allies who weathered obstacles to make institutional changes.

An Asset-Based Approach

I take an asset-based approach that addresses thriving and achieving (Arredondo, 2002; Comas-Díaz and Vázquez, 2018) to resist the status quo and to affirm capabilities, knowledge, and cultural capital. In *Presumed Incompetent* (Gutiérrez Muhs, Flores Niemann, González, and Harris, 2012), we hear the voices of women marginalized in university departments because they did not seem to fit or were otherwise considered nonworthy of being in the hallow halls of the academy. Living with double standards, discrimination, and other demeaning microaggressions are familiar to many women, particularly women with intersecting identities or visible ethnic/racial identity, that is being a member of a visible racial ethnic group (VERG) (Helms, 1990). Latinx women are automatically of VERG status, readily seen as tokens, and often engaged to give the lone voice to issues of diversity and other underrepresented issues. Over the years, I have been called upon to represent the woman, woman of color, or diversity point of view, and though I do not consider it a compliment, I know that to have a seat at the table, being that voice for diversity, is a fact of life in the academy. As one of the *lideres* stated, "If we are not present, ethnic minority student needs are often minimized and overlooked. Yes, it is tiring, but we have to be leader advocates."

The Borderlands Context for Latina Leaders

Representing multiple identity groups and also being true to one's mestiza (biracial, generally of indigenous and European heritages) self means a continuous dance of emotional and cognitive dissonance. Several terms from the social sciences describe the continuous borderlands experiences for Latina leaders. The *wild zone* metaphor (Candelaria, 1997) speaks to the chaos often experienced by Latinas in settings with double standards, challenges to their scholarship and way of being, deliberate questioning of their authority, and minimization of their accomplishments. Though this may sound unthinkable, these behaviors occur in academic units both for faculty and administrators, both overtly and covertly. In two different roles at PSI, a Latina leader had successes during financial crises.

She balanced the budget. However, when she had to eliminate lecturers, she was attacked by the faculty. "They accused me of behavior I did not recognize." If not experienced, a Latina can be caught off guard and vilified for doing her job. This accomplished leader persisted in the face of adversity.

"Nepantlera" is a concept coming from the Nahuatl word *nepantla*, advanced by Gloria Anzaldúa (2002) as a specific Latina identity. Essentially *nepantla* refers to being in between (Keating, 2006) and being boundary crossers, a borderlands experience. Another dimension of *nepantleras* is women's sense of being in constant displacement (Anzaldúa, 2002). For Latina administrators, navigating multiple in-between space becomes familiar and predictable. These spaces for situational leadership are with the faculty, administrators, colleagues, and other groups for which one holds responsibility. It is also a reflection of one's bicultural identity and bicognitive capacity for knowing how to work with a range of different individuals. Although being a *nepantlera* is a strength, because of the Latina's difference, "otherness" is often projected on her by men and/or majority women.

The concept of otherness was introduced in the feminist literature by Simone de Beauvoir (1952) who pointed out that the unequal relationships between women and men are a result of assumptions of women as being lesser than, the weaker sex. The concept has additional relevance for Latinas, categorized as ethnic minorities or simply minorities, another form of stigmatization. Multiple identities of difference or otherness are part of one's birthright but also affect power in relationships and, for Latina leaders, challenges to authority.

Women Leaders in the Academy

Percentage-wise, there has been an increase in women chancellors and presidents, predominantly white women, during the past ten years. It is fairly easy to point to women like Nancy Cantor at Rutgers in her second presidency. She was with Syracuse previously. The president of the University of Pennsylvania, Amy Guttman, has been in her position since 2004 and has been reappointed through 2022. Other white female presidents have served at multiple universities, an indication of their social capital and the way the system works to their benefit. Attendance at major higher education conferences gives visibility to the white female majority as deans, provosts, and chairs. Though space does not allow it, most white women presidents have attended Association of American Universities (AAU) whereas the Latina presidents, particularly those of Puerto Rican heritage, earned their bachelor's degree on the island or from a mainland public university. Perceptions and projections of Latina leaders' credentials is likely considered with respect to fit or suitability for particular senior administrative roles in PWI.

Will the Latina Leaders Stand Up?

A review of Latina women presidents was undertaken through the assistance of the American Association of Hispanics in Higher Education (AAHHE) and a few personal updates I made. Of the twenty-five women on their list, nine have been community college presidents. Several have held more than two presidencies. Only three have been presidents in private institutions. Shirley Collado, a psychologist with Dominican cultural roots, became president of Ithaca College in 2017. Contemporary presidents at flagship universities include Waded Cruzado of Puerto Rican heritage at Montana State University and Ana Maria Cauce of Cuban heritage at University of Washington. Two Latinas have been presidents at two public universities. These are France Cordova of Mexican heritage with University of California, Riverside, and Purdue, and Mildred Garcia of Puerto Rican heritage with California State, Dominguez Hills, and California State, Fullerton. One of the longest-serving presidents was Juliet Garcia of Mexican heritage and changemaker with the University of Texas-Brownsville. Space does not allow for identification of all women who have made contributions as academic leaders, community cultural brokers, and Latinx role models, yet in the future, all need to tell their story.

Structures and Climate Affecting Women Leaders

The culture of higher education is one of heteropatriarchy, whiteness, heterosexism, and upper-class privilege. It is the overlay that informs the structures and governing processes in universities and historically benefitted male professors and administrators. The chilly climate (Sandler and Hall, 1986), stereotype threat (Steele, 1999), and universities as psychic prisons (Morgan, 1997) are just a few of the dynamics that affect the retention of women and thereby their progress to leadership ranks. Power and privilege are in the hands primarily of white men, and as the literature has revealed, the men are preferred over women leaders. They are perceived to be a better fit or implicitly more prepared to lead (Eagly and Carli, 2007; Eagly and Chin, 2010). The leadership books in the public and academic domain are written primarily by white men. When women are authors or co-authors of higher education leadership books, the focus is on new frameworks for sensemaking of the university (Bolman and Gallos, 2011) or other structural frameworks to understand how it functions. These are valuable to those who go into higher education studies but may remain simply too theoretical if they do not point to the role of these structures to practices of exclusion based on gender, ethnicity, sexual orientation, and so forth. In other words, leadership books in higher education ignore the fact that institutions have structures that contribute to the success of the same select white men.

Stereotyping is a barrier and climate issue for women leaders in general. All women are stereotyped, as was illustrated in Kanter's (1977) classic book on men and women in organizations. At the time, the women's movement was underway, and sexual harassment legislation was emerging. The glass ceiling metaphor also emerged as a concept (1995) symbolizing how women cannot rise to the top, or the C-Suite, as it is called in the corporate world. Among the explanations were that the norms held for women were really about male behavior such as dominance, transactional behavior, and appearance (Cheung and Halpern, 2010; Eagly and Carli, 2007). Women are socialized to be part of a web, relationship-oriented, supportive, and agreeable versus disagreeable. Of course, these gender-bound behaviors were not seen as powerful and effective for effective leading and decision-making. Latina leaders are swept into these broad stereotyped attributes but also are viewed through specific racial/ethnic deficit lenses.

Expectations about educated and competent Latinas are still informed by stereotypes of entertainers, telenovela actresses, or anchors on Spanish-speaking networks (Arredondo, 2011). Though professionals, the latter dress often for what appears to be a social outing versus a professional assignment. The sexualization of Latinas continues, and this imagery is likely not easy to replace with that of a woman who dresses professionally and is all about business. One dean shared an example of relevance to this point. When interviewing for her first academic position in the Bible belt region, the male committee chair asked her, "Are you pure?"

Calmly she managed the micro-assault and sought clarification. She pointed out that the man had no experiences with lighter-skinned Latinas with a doctorate. All he imagined were stereotypes. She was hired, and he became her strongest advocate.

Further, because most university personnel have had few Latina colleagues or supervisors, it is the stereotyped images that likely dominate their views. Stereotyping about the "minority" in an organization is generally held by those with power (Fiske, 1993). In her research, Fiske found that those in control have the power to control stereotyping and that this has an impact on the individuals being stereotyped with respect to selection for leadership positions.

Whiteness and Niceness

For all women of color, the culture of whiteness is ever-present. The majority work in PWI, and quite often the woman of color integrates the department. Though being the first or the only one is generally not a new experience, for Latina leaders, it does require navigating with diplomacy, mistrust, and hypervigilance (Arredondo, 2011). Latinas have lower ascribed status than white women, regardless of their position. This is a parallel process to white men as the norm for women in general with respect to communication style, expressions of self-confidence, and attributed power. A white woman may be evaluated on her competence, but for Latinas and other women of color, there are low expectations because of their stereotyped identity status (Sanchez-Hucles and Davis, 2010; Arredondo, 2003). In short, Latinas do not have white privilege or a set of "unearned assets" (McIntosh, 1989). Every accomplishment must be earned.

Expectations of niceness are also held for Latinas—lots of smiles, friendliness, and even acquiescence. In a study of Latinas/os in educational and political settings, the concept of the "politics of niceness" emerged (Alemán, 2009). It was found that Latinas were expected to be considerate of others by being nice, respectful, and agreeable—not showing dissatisfaction with the status quo. With the stereotyped views of Latinas as subservient and inexperienced in the academy, questioning or, at worst, disagreeing may lead to labeling the woman as rude or not a team player or good fit. The double binds and double standards for Latinas and other women of color in the academy often are less than affirming of their intellectual talent (Eagly and Chin, 2010). Another dimension of academic life is the Latina's relationship with her supervisor. When one arrives in the role of chair, program director, dean, or even associate provost, more often than not, the supervisor is a white man or woman, inexperienced having a Latina colleague or supervisee of such high status. This can truly be a disadvantage that leads to patronizing behavior, over-monitoring, and undervaluation of the woman's leadership capabilities. When a supervisor demonstrates ambiguous empowerment (Turner, 2002) or public disrespect of any form, it will undermine the Latina's authority and make it more challenging to have her direct reports and colleagues see her as a leader. Several examples are shared in this chapter.

Leadership Paradigms

There is expansive leadership literature written primarily by white men in the corporate world, consultants, ex-CEOs, and so forth. Early work by McGregor (1960) discussed Theory X- and Theory Y-type male leaders, individuals who are autocratic and exert command-and-control style of behavior. The premise was that leaders' need for achievement and power would motivate them to be more authoritative and in control (McClelland, 1975). Alternatives to this top-down form of leading emerged and were described as situational leadership (Hersey, Blanchard, and Johnson, 2007), seen as a more person-centered approach and less transactional. The latter seem to reflect more female styles of leadership that also emerged. Not surprisingly, female styles referred to women's collectivistic and interactive styles, coach and teacher-like behavior that tends to be more people-centered and participatory (Eagly and Carli, 2007).

In short, leadership by women could be characterized as inclusive, transformative, and relational leadership.

Another perspective is that of organizational health. Lencioni (2012) proposes a four disciplines model with the first discipline being the building of a cohesive leadership team. To build the team, the leader must help individuals to develop trust, master conflict, commit to achievement, and embrace accountability. While the leader is the orchestra leader, she must also be a participant and balance the dual relationship with individuals she supervises. Lencioni (2012) describes the leader's capacity to promote organizational health as an advantage for well-being and performance within a department or the institution overall.

Indigenous leadership models are also of relevance to appreciating Latina styles of leading and are different from those of the mainstream models discussed. The Osah Gan Gio model (Johnson, 1997) was described as having five roles for leaders: "sharing a commitment to serve their community, claiming their voice for themselves and their community, demonstrated and modeled ways that education is key to cultural survival and self-determination, traveling across boundaries to understand and bridge relationships with others who are different from themselves, and continuously nurturing their inner spirit and sustaining their soul through balance in their lives" (Minthorn and Chávez, 2015, p. 3). These role expectations reflect the *nepantlera* concept previously discussed (Anzaldúa, 2002) of women crossing boundaries with no specific identity other than to do the work at hand. Further Indigenous ways of knowing fundamentally are relational; learning is communal and emerges in relation to one another or others. This is a very non-Western worldview because in Eurocentric leadership models, even if relational leadership is practiced, rarely is there mention of shared ways of knowledge development. The leader still operates in a vertical versus horizontal position in relation to her unit. The Indigenous process also involves storytelling, aligning with the approach in this chapter. Herein, narratives or *testimonios* were invited to give voice to our Latina leaders.

Another mainstream paradigm of relevance to learning about and from Latina leaders is the theory of emotional intelligence (EI) (Goleman, 1995) and how it applies to leaders. The EI model has four domains that seem very similar to what we teach in multicultural counseling and communications skills. These are self-awareness, self-management, social awareness, and relationship management. The self-awareness domain, as with the multicultural counseling paradigm, is most critical because it enables empathy and self-management. The more conscious leaders are of their biases and assumptions and who and what pushes their hot buttons, the more likely they will be able to manage relationships effectively and express empathy (Goleman, Boyatzis, and McKee, 2002). In many respects, the domains of EI are what are called soft skills and generally associated with women, not men. However, successful leadership is highly relational and people-centered, and accordingly empathy engenders resonance.

With resonant leadership, individuals perform from their values and evoke emotions of people around them. The leader can prolong the positive emotions they arouse through their encouraging and attentive behavior (Goleman et al., 2002). The counter behavior is dissonant leadership, which evokes emotionally discordant group behavior because of the leader's less than affirming and relational style.

Introducing leadership paradigms that are considered mainstream will put into context what I learned about these Latina's leadership mindset and practices. Though their ethnic and gender identity differs from that of the typical white female and male administrator in higher education, their approaches to leading primarily reflect relational and resonant leadership. Power and authority are invoked but also informed by their cultural models, values, and ethics.

Culture-Centered Approaches to Inquiring and Learning

This chapter specifically addresses Latina academic leadership by attending to the literature on women leaders, culture (Latinx)-specific concepts relative to Latinas and our worldviews for being and engaging, and Latinas "ways of knowing" as *mujeristas* navigating the borderlands. To learn more about Latina ways of knowing and practices as leaders, I considered more holistic and culture-centered approaches. The Multicultural Guidelines (APA, 2003) suggest "understanding the need to incorporate cultural context into research questions" (p. 81) and the use of "culturally appropriate assessment tools and practices" (p. 132) when conducting research. Though the narratives used are not drawn from a research study per se, the two approaches, *testimonio* and appreciative inquiry, contribute to knowledge-building.

Appreciative Inquiry

Originally formulated by David Cooperrider (1987), appreciative inquiry is described as a collaborative and highly participatory process. Adding to this is a definition referring to appreciative inquiry as an approach that focuses on "strengths, vision and hope for the future" (Coghlan, Preskill, and Catsambas, 2003, p. 5). Another description is that appreciative inquiry is about inquiry as intervention (Cooperrider and Whitney, 2005). The questionnaire that informs the narratives invited the women to reflect on experiences as leaders, influencing forces, and the effects of their leadership on others and their unit of responsibility.

Testimonio

In the classic text, *The Maria Paradox* (Gil and Vazquez, 1997), the Ten Commandments of Marianismo first appear. The *mandamientos*, or commandments, suggest that Latinas must suffer in silence as dutiful mothers and caretakers, in particular. The lack of voice is apparent in these ten rules many Latinas learned growing up. *Testimonio*, on the other hand, is about sharing to raise consciousness that the Latina is not alone in patriarchal, racist, and oppressive organizations; others know of what she speaks. "*Testimonio* is fluid, including an individual strategy as well as a collective method. A single voice in *testimonio* goes beyond an individual occurrence, expressing the experience of many oppressed individuals" (Comas-Díaz and Vazquez, 2018, p. 5). Capturing the voices of Latinas is applying their *testimonio* for collective benefit.

Gathering *Testimonios*

In preparation for this chapter, I invited ten Latinx academic leaders to share their perspectives and experiences from different positions in the academy. Eight responded. My goal was to take a strengths-based, appreciative inquiry approach, inquiring about the mind-set they applied as leaders. In other words, how did they think about the portfolio and situations for which they were accountable? I also asked about sources of courage and persistence to manage adversity and to use their authority effectively. Another question was about managing macro/microaggressions or other interpersonal challenges. Latina leaders are often rendered invisible as women of color; thus negative projections and stereotypes about their competence in these positions are commonplace (Arredondo, 2011). Again I inquired about how they walked the borderlands in the midst of others' conscious and unconscious stereotypes and verbal and nonverbal behavior aggressions.

Insomuch as all of the women are Latinas, I wanted to learn about the role of their Latina identity and heritage in enacting leadership roles. Finally these Latina leaders recognize their singularity and want to see others advance and succeed; thus their recommendations for future leaders are noteworthy.

These were empowered women, generally the first Latina in their position, all pioneers of sorts in PWIs with a couple of exceptions. For the women from HSIs, there were similar and different experiences, with different lessons to impart. They accepted the opportunity to participate because they recognize their unique positions as Latinas and want to give back.

Latina Leaders in Action

The eight women who shared their perspectives on leading have been academic administrators from three to seventeen years, and in the academy on average twenty-five years. Those in universities that offer tenure are tenured (seven), primarily full professors, and the majority have held multiple administrative assignments. For example, one woman was a chair, associate provost, and dean; another was a chair and founding college dean. A third was department chair and institution-wide administrator. The woman with the most years of administrative experience had been a senior vice provost, vice provost, dean, chair, director, and principal investigator for a $14 million, six-year federal grant. At least three of the leaders had been founding department chairs, and the majority were from the field of psychology. Two of the women were with HSIs, and six were at PWIs. Six of the women were of Mexican American heritage, and two were Puerto Rican. Anecdotally, all are bilingual.

Mind-set for Leading

Quite often, leadership is discussed as it relates to style—relational, transactional, authoritative, transpersonal, and so forth. The women expressed lived knowledge about the interdependence of awareness, knowledge, and skills or behaviors, outlined in the multicultural counseling competency models (Arredondo et al., 1996) as how they led and supervised. The premise is that thinking informs emotions and behaviors; thus the opening interview question was, *What is your mind-set when facing a challenging situation, and what are the sources for this way of thinking?*

The challenging situations described, by and large, involved changes in one's unit such as restructuring, eliminating staff and/or an entire program area, and following new business protocols because of a merger. One woman spoke of her mind-set as being one of "relentless pursuit of excellence," a "generational family resource" in the midst of multiple changes occurring simultaneously. She thought about a mentor and how this university president had managed adversities. Recalling her mentor's pragmatic, caring approach helped to ground her. Another leader discussed relying on her cultural upbringing in a bilingual/bicultural environment on the Mexico/U.S. border. The daily borderlands experiences meant she was regularly applying her cultural capital and knowledge to negotiate day-to-day life situations, and this meant often taking the "high road." When things did not go her way, she thought about the *dicho* (saying), *Cada loco con su tema*, in other words, "to each their own" or "different strokes for different folks," and followed through with her responsibilities.

The leaders also commented about the confusion and emotional dissonance they felt when facing these challenging situations and how important it was to seek consultation from individuals who were trustworthy and objective. Some of these individuals were outside of the institution with no stake in the given situation, but they cared about their colleague and offered sage advice. Recognizing their internal stress, the women also worked collaboratively with others on their team to not be so isolated. As one leader stated, "Maintaining a positive attitude and believing that it can be resolved is half the battle."

Several women cited the use of facts and data, including best practices to represent their position. No one spoke of managing from a gut feeling in spite of the upset she was experiencing. In all examples, the women thought about how to resolve the challenge in front of them pragmatically. Because of their position, some leaders could recognize the forthcoming issues before others knew about them. With this foresight, they applied the belief that it is best "to address issues before they become challenging." As such, transparency with one's team was their modus operandi. One leader mentioned that sharing information about an organizational dilemma allows for working together "to identify possible solutions."

Also part of their mind-set was awareness of the stereotypical ways in which Latinas are viewed as "too emotional, over-expressive, loud, and inexperienced." As a visible administrator, the stakes are high, as was cited previously. As a result, the leaders maintained their business poise and remained in charge. From their accounts, they read situations well because they knew the bicultural context, engaged in perspective-taking, and applied their EI.

There was consistency among the examples shared, suggesting that Latina leaders have a DNA of sorts for approaching challenging situations. Having focus, providing consultation, maintaining a positive attitude, recalling guiding principles from one's upbringing such as *dichos*, researching best practices, and staying true to one's values were woven through the predominant responses.

Sources for Courage, Deliberateness, and Persistence

Building off the first question, the women were asked to reflect on their sources for courage, deliberateness, and persistence in the midst of adversity. The most common responses pointed to family members, women, particularly mothers who demonstrated their strength in the midst of adversity their daughters had never experienced. One leader, at the age of fifteen, witnessed her mother's determination when her father died. Consistently, her mother modeled behaviors to ensure all was provided just as before. Her resourcefulness stood out to her daughter, and as she became a leader, these examples of finding alternatives and self-reliance remains with her. She also recalled the network of *familia* and friends, women who remained single when they lost their spouse and exhibited "strong values, sense of worth and integrity not found in many formally schooled individuals."

"My family history of strong, assertive, and resilient women has served me as role models for how to stand up for myself and especially to advocate for those I represent," commented another leader. Consistently I heard counter-narratives to the weaknesses of women described in the Ten Commandments of Marianismo (Gil and Vazquez, 1997). The leaders admired and incorporated the strengths of Latina mothers, grandmothers, and tías, icons they recalled when pushing through hostility and disruptions in the workplace. The same leader spoke about the aggressiveness toward her leadership versus that of her predecessor, a white male. She knew that losing departmental space was going to affect her entire unit and took the steps, including open communication with her colleagues, to stand firm. Protecting one's department or team came up in various comments, underlining the collectivistic approach of these Latinas.

An associate dean and former department chair pointed to her mother as her biggest source of emotional and pragmatic support. In fact, she often used her mother as a consultant, valuing her know-how as the leader of large governmental agencies, a woman who had major management responsibilities but who was also the target of discrimination by her staff and administration. "People frequently asked to work with *someone who was not Mexican*" like her mother, but her mother always took the road of dignity and self-respect, sprinkled with humor. Thus her daughter turned to her mother for consultation on daily employee behaviors when she moved into a new position because she trusted her experience and judgment. In fact, she goes on to explain that when the leadership team was stumped about the problem, "the dean would ask me to call my mother and we would put her on speakerphone so she could discuss particular issues with her." Her mother's advice was always deemed practical and knowledgeable, particularly about state law and workplace ethics.

A university-wide administrator and former founding chair shared that it was her parents' work ethic that inculcated in her a respect for hard work and support for one another. She witnessed how they taught by doing and corrected by modeling. Moreover, she added, "As Mexican immigrants, we brought a very strong sense of *respeto al projimo*," or respect for the other. "I think that women of color organize, manage, create, and inspire based upon cultural values," stated a Latina dean. She went on to say that along with her supervisor, also a woman of color of Asian heritage, they operated from the belief of elevating the work of the group versus the individual and that together they led through collaboration and cohesion. Their shared leadership approach also demonstrates the Latinx style of interdependence and being *comadres*—life co-mothers (Comas-Díaz and Vazquez, 2018).

Another leader indicated that she deliberately connects with her *familia* to keep her balanced and grounded. After all, her *familia* has always been the center of her life. She has consistently done this outreach and will continue to do so for her benefit and theirs. In a similar vein, another leader mentioned that dinnertime talks with her young sons are about her day, both the ups and downs of a microaggression, such as confusing her for another woman of color. She wants them to feel connected to what she does and to educate them about these real-world occurrences. In so doing, she experiences their support and appreciation.

Of course trustworthy friends and colleagues, respected supervisors, and other persons of color, particularly women, can be allies and supports during the challenging times. One leader had multiple examples of a previous supervisor who had faced extensive adversity in her years as a university president. Recalling the president's thoughtful and thorough approaches inspired her to persist when situations became challenging. One leader remembered "César Chávez drinking chamomile tea before going in to negotiate with the farm owners so he could stay calm." This image gave her encouragement to remain firm and persistent in negotiating and defending the situation of losing space; she prevailed.

Most Gratifying and Least Gratifying Experiences as an Administrator

Most Gratifying

Descriptions of most gratifying experiences generally focused on others and the benefits of initiatives and resulting changes initiated and encouraged by the Latina leaders. These initiatives were for increasing student benefits and resources, staff professional development, and institutional changes to increase diversity. Evident in the responses were examples of leadership that reached many. None mentioned gratification that was "me-focused." No one said, "I felt accomplished by what resulted" or "I was really satisfied with the outcome of my initiatives." The language was about the other, about the collective good. A few examples follow.

Several Latinas addressed their intentionality to increase diversity in their unit, particularly focused on changes in the faculty ranks. How they went about leading the charge was also noteworthy. They described coalescing team members to agree to pursue the course of increasing diversity in the organization. One dean stated that she realized that in order to attract diverse faculty, she had to have a critical mass of the faculty, regardless of their ethnic backgrounds supporting the diversity goal. She required that all faculty searches include a statement that candidates "demonstrate a commitment to diversity as evidenced in their research, teaching, or engagement efforts." Moreover, she personally reviewed the records of candidates who would be invited to campus interviews. If they did not have evidence to meet the diversity criteria, they were not approved for an interview. As a result of holding firm to her expectations about diversity, there was an increase in the number of faculty "involved in researching diversity issues, as did the inclusion of diversity content in coursework." The success of the diversity requirement language for searches in her unit became a model for the campus at-large. Before long, the entire campus required similar language in their search announcements.

A department chair endeavored to increase faculty diversity and accomplished a fifty-fifty ratio. She knew that her department was committed to diversity in action and wanted to achieve parity and that it was her role as their leader to support this goal. She also recognized that there might be barriers from institutional leaders because of this bold, independent action taken by the faculty; thus she had to run interference to support their actions. Not everything went smoothly in spite of the deliberate goal. She reported that at times, searches were paused if there were not enough diverse candidates in the pool of applicants. The process required "patience, outreach strategy, and negotiation," and they accomplished their goal of parity among the eighteen faculty and six staff.

Staying with the departmental focus, another dean described her satisfaction in building a unit and its efficacy. Because she had the opportunity to establish the unit from the ground up, she could apply her knowledge and previous experiences to ensure that functions and efficient operating procedures versus personalities grounded the unit. She described with pride how she held the staff, including student workers, to higher standards than most units, including that of the president's office. What is telling with this example and others about "shaping" professional behavior is that it seems to derive from the Latina leaders own cultural upbringing. The *respeto al projimo* value and examples from mothers and parents about dignified demeanor seemed evident. In the Latinx culture, parents are expected to raise children who are *buen educados* or well-mannered (Arredondo, Gallardo Cooper, and Zapata, 2014). This value also seems to be evident in the leaders' examples.

Building or establishing programs was another gratifying administrative experience. One leader who had been both a chair and a dean described her success in building two graduate programs in mental health counseling, at two different institutions. Both programs are designed to receive the gold standard accreditation of the Council for the Accreditation of Counseling and Related Educational Programs (CACREP). She noted that this accomplishment in a PWI with very few ethnic minority leaders and faculty was very satisfying. Additional gratifying experiences for her were providing opportunities for faculty and staff to engage in professional development opportunities. By prioritizing continuing education, she was encouraging and mentoring her direct reports on new possibilities and to aspire. As with two other deans' examples, this Latina leader took pride in creating an inclusive environment, one that increased the hiring of diverse faculty and staff and increased the enrollment of diverse graduate students.

A graduate dean was most proud of her leadership that led to positive outcomes for graduate students. Among these were increasing stipends, creating award programs for recognizing achievements of faculty and students alike, shepherding the establishing of a Phi Kappa Psi chapter to recognize upper division and graduate students for their academic achievements, and creating space for students to engage and study together.

The senior vice provost identified institutional shortcomings that led to important improvements for the university. For example, she led revisions of policies that were out of compliance with accreditors, supported deans to increase hiring faculty of color, assisted Latinx faculty to develop a Latinx studies program, and implemented changes that increased freshmen enrollment by 3 percent, thereby improving the institutional budget. She was insightful and proactive. This Latina also compiled data that validated grievances from women about a hostile work climate and prepared a report about salary, hiring, and retention inequities specific to women and women of color. "These successes were challenging but invigorating, as they were in line with my mission to effect change toward social justice." Sadly, when a new president was hired, he asked her to step back to faculty and told her that people complained because she seemed only to care about people of color.

Latina leaders' skills often meant assuming multiple roles and responsibilities that can initially be gratifying. One such talented leader, despite her youth, was assigned two senior-level administrative roles by her university president who had confidence in her capabilities. One of her assignments was to create a new academic advising center for the newly restructured HSI. This led to partnerships for best practices for an advising center and deliberate goals for excellence, which was her modus operandi. As a result, the center became an often-cited "national model of a contemporary academic advising."

When her university merged with another institution, she was charged to chair the new combined counseling department and, of course, the CACREP accreditation process. This task required her best collaboration and negotiation skills, as well as her values for integrity and cultural competence. She had learned well from the president who mentored her, and this gave her to lead the new endeavors.

Least Gratifying and Disappointments

The most gratifying examples serve to point to the Latina leaders' mindset for planning, goal-orientation, high expectations, and student, faculty, and staff-centeredness. They approached their roles and responsibilities with affirmative intentions to improve the environment, to increase diversity, and to apply best practices with integrity and care. Thus, the disappointments and challenging situations indicate that in spite of high-level intentions and leadership acumen, other factors or individuals intervene that are out of one's control.

The talented Latina who was charged with establishing the advising center and chairing the counseling program learned that her pursuit of excellence for historically underserved students was not embraced by her new colleagues. In fact, it was met with resistance. Where she had an entrepreneurial and twelve-hours-per-day, seven-days-a-week work ethic, when it came to the merger of her institution with another, she quickly encountered some unmovable forces. First, new colleagues and administrators wanted to maintain the status quo from their institution, and because it was the bigger "dog," they prevailed. The advising center was left understaffed by overtaxed workers, and students found advisors, primarily temporary workers, who were not prepared to meet their needs for support and counsel. Lacking resources and personnel made it impossible for her to continue in the role with dignity. She decided to step down from her position of counseling department chair when the dean asked her to falsify accreditation documents. Though she preferred to stay in the leadership role, she could not abide by unethical behavior. To this day, three years later, she wonders if she could have done something different to maintain standards she was used to applying. Her answer to herself is "no," and she goes on to say that she found "more individuals fighting for mediocrity than those interested in doing the hard work." She has acknowledged that these were life-changing experiences and with pride looks forward to continuing her ancestral (Latinx) and professional legacy with the lessons learned about flexibility, grit, and resilience.

Another least gratifying experience was shared by a former dean, now a department chair for the third time. She found herself, as has happened with other Latina leaders, working for an administrator that had not hired them due to a reorganization. The values for diversity of the original supervisor were not supported by her new boss in a meaningful way; it was more lip service. Faculty and staff saw right through this demeanor, creating tension among the few faculty and staff of color. Many of these individuals hired during the Latina dean's administration left. Senior administrators did not support her. In fact, she felt devalued and powerless to effect change for equity and diversity. Within a year, she resigned.

Though there were more examples of satisfying experiences, the least satisfying ones are disheartening and show a cost to the institution and the individual. It is obvious that there are limits to a Latina leader's efficacy to advance change on behalf of underserved students and to improve the diversity among faculty and staff when one's authority is undermined. When the lack of support comes from the top, the woman has few options. She can play by the rules or leave in order to uphold her ethics, maintain mental well-being, and thrive again.

The senior vice provost found herself assuming leadership roles with two PWIs with serious financial challenges. In 2008, at the height of the U.S. financial crisis, she stepped into the role of college dean with a large public institution. The only person of color in administration, she was instructed to address a million-dollar deficit for her college. Through painstaking diligence, she was able to make the reduction and maintain all academic programs and tenure-track faculty, although she had to cut some popular lecturers. As a result of this one action, some faculty rebelled and blamed her. Unfortunately she was not backed up by the provost who had hired her; he asked her to step down and offered her a vice provost position.

When this Latina assumed the position of senior vice provost at another PWI, she once again found a financial crisis. It surprised her because when she was interviewed for the position and inquired about the institution's financial situation, she had not been informed of the crisis at hand. Once again, she became engaged in budget-cutting, an action that did not set well with faculty or staff. Nevertheless she persisted and led important outcomes for the university.

The Use of Authority in Challenging Situations

Four of the leaders discussed experiences where their authority was questioned, sabotaged, or ignored. Several poignant examples come from an associate dean in academic affairs and a former chair in a psychology program and the director of a social science unit. Being the first women of color in the role led to hostile and undermining reactions from others.

The associate dean assumed a position following a woman who had worked her way to the top over twenty years and earning her doctorate along the way. The department she inherited was white and heterosexual. Her supervisor, the graduate dean, was an Asian American woman. Though unusual, there were two women of color appointed to lead a graduate school. The first evidence of undermining came from a white male who everyone assumed would have become the associate dean. However, he did not have the credentials and was not a candidate; still perhaps the memory of the previous associate dean who worked her way to the top stood out, and the staff began to go to him for advice and supervision. The fact that he allowed this behavior was evidence of his lack of support for his new colleague and supervisor. He went so far as to advise her to not speak up at faculty meetings because the previous dean had rarely offered an opinion. Silencing women and women of color is a common practice (Kanter, 1977). Several other blatant incidents occurred; among these were open hostile statements about American Indian students and insubordination—withholding information from her. These incidents represented decision points of how to best manage and assume her authority. As the Latina leader indicated, she had to address the intentional mistreatment and sabotage. With each offender, she took a nonconfrontational but a firm approach to review the incident and request an explanation. From there, she stated clear expectations for the individual's future behavior. Another tact was to prepare a summary of each discussion and the development of a performance improvement plan. She made it clear that the transgression required remediation. Another response was to provide staff training by the Office of Equity. With this, everyone had the same message about workplace behavior that was expected.

This systematic, level-headed approach gave staff choices. Out of eleven, four left because they could not abide by the behavior change required or chose to retire. Two went so far as to file complaints against her with the Office of Equity that were dismissed as groundless. Our Latina leader persisted alongside the dean, and upon their departure, they could point to a high-functioning unit, inclusive of a staff that was 30 percent diverse.

Managing Adversity and Microaggressions—Recommendations

The previous discussions have addressed the topics about managing adversity and microaggressions in some ways, but there was also a specific question about recommendations based on one's leadership experiences. Once again, the Latina leaders described pragmatic, straightforward actions. An associate dean indicated that she addressed microaggression in the moment directly and generally with a sense of humor. She provided a salient sexist example that likely occurs for many women. She observed that a male co-worker always complimented her when she wore dresses. Her tact was to bring this to awareness by asking if he realized that he only complimented here when she wore a dress.

"What do you think I should make of that?" she asked.

The question disarmed him because she let him know, with a smile, that she observed his behavior.

Being confused with other women of color often occurs for Latinas even if we do not look like the person with whom we are confused. A Latina director wrote about instances when supervisors called her by the wrong name, that of another woman of color. Ironically, she mentions, this never occurred when she was a junior faculty, but now in an administrative role, it occurs. Her response was to remain calm and share with the other person her name. At times, others accepted the correction and were apologetic, opening an opportunity for a valuable discussion. Of course, there were individuals who became defensive, and the Latina, if not careful, could have ended up taking care of the offender because of "white fragility." She recommended being nonreactionary but responsive, expressing emotional intelligence. Another avenue recommended was to share microaggressions and macroaggressions with certain colleagues of color for they too have similar experiences.

In the daily administrative grind, long stressful days are common because of deadlines, multiple meetings, and budget planning. Being an administrator for these Latinas was more like a 24/7 work life. Thus, all cited planned self-care as essential. This included celebrating victories at work, looking at the upside of outcomes and not just the remaining challenges, and taking time out with team members to relax. They described self-care as a necessity, not a luxury, and recommended ways to relieve stress through working out, getting a massage, exercising, disconnecting from technology for short periods of time, and hanging out with *familia* or friends. A former dean recommended the use of a "dammit doll" to let out pent-up emotions.

Another chair noted that now that she is aware of microaggressions and their prevalence in the workplace. She also recognizes that it is almost impossible to counter them at every turn. Thus, she decided to invite a friend to co-create with her a work environment for thriving. Together they initiated a support group for women of color staff and faculty with monthly meetings, open to whomever could participate virtually. The virtual platform allows for women in other locations or someone who works remotely. In keeping with the collectivistic approach, the Latina leader and her colleague have facilitated the "owning" of the group by all of the women by rotating responsibility for leading discussions and surfacing topics of interest. In little time, the group has twenty-five active members.

One of the deans shared that it was her years of experience in the academy that gave her the confidence to rise above situations of adversity. She offered two strategies she has used in times of challenge. Her first recommendation is to choose one's battles. Reacting to all microaggressions would be tiresome at best. She also recommended the importance of considering what is at stake before reacting or getting swept into the possible maelstrom. She offered a familiar situation that occurs when a woman, a Latina leader, is in a meeting with all men. She noted that predictably her opinions or contributions were being dismissed and those of the men were being entertained, although they were more like hers.

At the appropriate moment, she interrupted and took charge, saying, "Thank you, Tom, Dick and Harry. I made the very same observation five minutes ago, so it sounds like we are all in agreement."

By remaining calm and positive, she wrote, your authority comes through without sounding defensive. Thus, she moved on to other business or to end the meeting.

When and How Did You Arrive at a Place of "Satisfaction" With Yourself and Your Career Expectations?

Some of the Latina leaders with longer tenure as faculty and administrators reflected on this question and shared straightforward thoughts. One dean with a tenure of ten years saw the fruits of her student-focused goals through their accomplishments. She noted the numerous graduation and induction ceremonies that brought together *familias* to celebrate achievements of family members, the majority of whom were first-generation college students. As a result of her experiences as an administrator, she also came to the conclusion that she did not have aspirations to become a provost or a president.

Another dean, also with ten years of experience, found that feedback on her annual and administrative reviews were sources of reflection and satisfaction. Through these reviews, she was able to see the goals she had set, her progress toward achieving these, and any changes she had to make. At the end of her ten-year tenure, there was a clear and objective means by which she and others could see the outcomes of her performance.

The Role of One's Latina Identity and Culture as a Source of Strength and Resilience

Women responded to this question directly and indirectly. References to *dichos*, family modeling of values and a strong work ethic when discussing other items, and examples of how they led by thinking about the collective good were most indirect ways the women responded to this item. The power of one's Latina identity came through the words of one department chair who stated that at an early age she was emboldened by her parents' encouragement and *coraje* (anger) about Mexican versus American history. She found more role models outside of her parents in Martha Bernal, the first Mexican American psychologist; Dolores Huerta, civil rights activist; and Melba Vazquez, the first Latina president of the American Psychological Association. She saw herself in all of these women. She also reported that involvement in the National Latinx Psychological Association and the National Multicultural Summits were particularly empowering.

A Latina dean gained awareness of her Latinidad when she stepped out of the culturally embedded community in which she grew up. However, as a result of her bilingual upbringing and her tendency to be an observer, she realized she had the foundation for leading and being in the world of the academy. She is proud of her upbringing and questions the behavior of other Latinas who play the race card or engage in bullying tactics. "I am embarrassed for us," she says and wonders what experiences caused them to "behave this way."

Another Latina dean stated she was proud of her Puerto Rican heritage and credited her mother for instilling a sense of pride and connection to her Latina and Puertorriqueña cultural background. Her mother set expectations for her about going to college, reminding her that education was a means to independence as a woman and that no one could take away her education. As a professional, she has become a leader in the NLPA, and as she contributes to the organization's growth, she finds that it "nourishes my soul and makes me a stronger and resilient person." Finally transmitting the culture is part of her responsibility as a Latina mamá and abuela. As her mother did, she wants to instill a sense of pride for their Puerto Rican heritage in her daughters and grandchildren. Moreover, she wants to live out her mother's encouragement about being independent by serving as a role model of resilience, independence, and power for her daughters.

Concluding Thoughts

> What kept me going was believing that I was making a difference in matters of equity and justice—for faculty, staff, and students.
> (Senior Provost)

The voices of Latina higher education administrators have shone a bright light on their courage, deliberateness, persistence, and pragmatic mindset. These are leaders applying EI and resonant leadership practices as they lead and manage diverse faculty and staff in order to meet important goals and achievements on behalf of their units and the institution. They draw from their cultural heritage and proudly affirm lessons learned from parents, mothers in particular, and other Latina models and icons outside of the *familia*.

I intentionally prepared this chapter to illustrate positively how Latinas facilitate change, make decisions, and manage adversity through an appreciative inquiry lens. Appreciative inquiry focuses on "strengths, visions, and hopes for the future" (Coghlan et al., 2003, p. 5). Thus the eight questions invited the women to reflect on the hows and whys of their practices, their ways of thinking and knowing how to respond to insubordination and sabotage, coalescing a team to advance diversity goals, build programs, and make their units look good. Some noted new realizations about their thinking in managing work situations or the influences of role models on how they consciously/unconsciously conducted themselves. In other words, the questions provoked an appreciation about how they drew upon cultural values and lived experiences as Latinas to walk the borderlands and to apply culture-centered resonant leadership.

When a Latina is selected for a senior administrative assignment, she is choosing to be there, and these women described the mind-set they applied to plan and manage cogently and affirmatively. They were ready to be leaders. At the same time, there were sticky patches and *desafíos* (challenges) of resistance in many forms, but they persevered and relied on trusted colleagues, friends, and *familia* in times of difficulty or perhaps as one dean indicated, turning to her mother who had extensive experiences leading organizations. These Latina leaders are roles models for all women for their application of cultural competencies, EI, resonant leadership, and ways of knowing. We can learn so much from their *testimonios* and share some specific recommendations they offered.

- Specific to relationships, they suggest alliances with other Latinas and women, particularly women of color, not to complain or air their frustrations, but to build a network of support, empowerment, and levity.
- Inform others of how you want to be seen by taking charge, setting limits, and being assertive with the administrative authority you hold.
- Recognize that as Latinas, you are often pigeonholed as only caring about diversity matters; others cannot see you beyond their stereotypes.
- Your personal integrity will be challenged because of a possible clash of your personal and institutional values.
- Address issues before they become challenges through people-centered outreach and engagement, such as "Breakfast with the Dean."
- If something makes you feel uncertain, ask yourself why. Is it an unknown area making you fearful because of a lack of experience? If so, reach out for advice or mentorship.
- Recognize that you have options to find environments where you will feel valued and thrive.

References

Alemán, Jr., E. (2009). Through the prism of critical race theory: Niceness and Latina/o leadership in the politics of education. *Journal of Latinos and Education*, 8(4), 290–311.

Anzaldúa, G. E. (1987). *Borderlands: La frontera: The new mestizo*. San Francisco, CA: Aunt Lute.

Anzaldúa, G. E (2002). Now let us shift . . . the path of *conocimiento* . . . inner work, public acts. In G. E. Anzaldúa and A. L. Keating (Eds.), *The bridge we call home: Radical visions for transformation* (pp. 540–570). New York, NY: Routledge.

American Psychological Association. (2003). Guidelines on multicultural education, training, research, practice and organizational change for psychologists. *American Psychologist*, 58, 377–402.

Arredondo, P. (2002). Mujeres Latinas-Santas y Marquesas. *Cultural Diversity and Ethnic Minority Psychology*, 8, 1–12.

Arredondo, P. (2003). Resistance to multiculturalism in organizations. In J. S. Mio and G. Y. Iwamasa (Eds.), *Multicultural mental health research and resistance: Continuing challenges of the new millennium* (pp. 83–104). New York, NY: Brunner-Routledge.

Arredondo, P. (2011). The "borderlands" experience for women of color as higher education leaders. In J. L. Martin (Ed.), *Women as leaders in education: Succeeding despite inequity, discrimination, and other challenges* (pp. 275–298). Westport, CT: Praeger Press.

Arredondo, P., Gallardo Cooper, M., and Zapata, A. (2014). *Culturally responsive situational counseling with Latinos.* Alexandria, VA: American Counseling Association.

Arredondo, P., Toporek, R., Brown, S. P., Jones, J., Locke, D. C., Sanchez, J., and Stadler, H. (1996). Operationalization of the multicultural counseling competencies. *Journal of Multicultural Counseling and Development,* 24, 42–78.

Bolman, L. G., and Gallos, J. V. (2011). *Reframing academic leadership.* San Francisco, CA: McGraw-Hill.

Candelaria, C. C. (1997). "The wild zone" thesis as gloss in Chicana literary study. *Feminisms: An anthology of literary theory and criticism* (Rev. ed., pp. 248–263). Brunswick, NJ: Rutgers University Press.

Cheung, F. M., and Halpern, D. F. (2010). Women at the top. *American Psychologist,* 65, 182–193.

Coghlan, A. T., Preskill, H., and Catsambas, T. T. (Eds.). (2003). *An overview of appreciative inquiry in evaluation.* New directions for evaluation, no. 100. San Francisco, CA: Josey-Bass.

Comas-Díaz, L., and Vazquez, C. I. (Eds.). (2018). *Latina psychologists thriving in the cultural borderlands.* New York, NY: Routledge.

Cooperrider, D. (1987). Appreciative inquiry in organizational life. *Research in Organizational Change and Development,* 1(1), 9–169.

Cooperrider, D. L., and Whitney, D. (2005). *A positive revolution in change: Appreciative inquiry.* Retrieved from www.researchgate.net/publication/237404587

de Beauvoir, S. (1952/1949). *The second sex.* (H. M. Parshley. Ed and Trans). Harmondsworth: Penguin.

Eagly, A. H., and Carli, L. L. (2007). *Through the labyrinth.* Boston, MA: Harvard Business School Press.

Eagly, A. H., and Chin, J. L. (2010). Diversity and leadership in a changing world. *American Psychologist,* 65, 216–224.

Federal Glass Ceiling Commission. (1995, November). *Solid investments: Making full use of the nation's human capital* (pp. 13–15). Washington, DC: U.S. Department of Labor.

Fiske, S. (1993). Controlling other people: The impact of power on stereotyping. *American Psychologist,* 48(6), 621–628.

Gil, R. M., and Vazquez, C. I. (1997). *The Maria paradox: How Latinas can merge old world traditions with new world self-esteem.* New York, NY: Perigee.

Goleman, D. (1995). *Emotional intelligence.* New York, NY: Bantam Books.

Goleman, D., Boyatzis, R., and McKee, A. (2002). *Primal leadership.* Boston, MA: HBS Press.

Gutierrez y Muhs, G., Niemann, Y. F., Gonzalez, C. G., Harris, A. P. (Eds.). (2012). *Presumed incompetent: The intersections of race and class for women in academia.* Logan, UT: University of Utah Press.

Helms, J. E. (Ed.). (1990). *Black and white racial identity attitudes: Theory, research and practice.* Westport, CT: Greenwood.

Hersey, P., Blanchard, K., and Johnson, D. E. (2007). *Management of organizational behavior: Leading human resources.* New York, NY: Prentice Hall.

Johnson, V. (1997). Weavers of change: Portraits of native American women educational leaders. *Dissertation Abstracts International, 59*(1), 36A.

Kanter, R. M. (1977). *Men and women of the corporation.* New York, NY: Basic Books.

Keating, A. L. (2006). From borderlands and new *mestizas* to nepantlas and nepantleras: Anzaldúan theories for social change. *Human Architecture: Journal of the Sociology of Self-Knowledge, 4*(3). Special Issue, 5–16.

Lencioni, P. (2012). *The advantage.* San Francisco, CA: Jossey-Bass.

McClelland, D. (1975). *Power: The inner experience.* New York, NY: John Wiley.

McGregor, D. (1960). *The human side of enterprise.* New York, NY: McGraw-Hill.

McIntosh, P. (1989, July/August). White privilege: Unpacking the invisible knapsack. *Peace and Freedom,* 8–10.

Minthorn, R. S., and Chávez, A. F. (Eds.). (2015). *Indigenous leadership in higher education.* New York, NY: Routledge.

Morgan, G. (1997). *Images of organization* (2nd ed.). Thousand Oaks, CA: Sage.

Sanchez-Hucles, J. V., and Davis, D. D. (2010). Women and women of color in leadership: Complexity, identity, and intersectionality. *American Psychologist, 65*(3), 171–181.

Sandler, B. L., and Hall, R. M. (1986). *The campus climate revisited: Chilly for women faculty, administrators, and graduate students.* Washington, DC: Association of American Colleges, Project on the Status and Education of Women.

Steele, C. M. (1999). Thin Ice: "Stereotype threat" and black college students. *The Atlantic Monthly, 284*(2), 44–47, 50–54.

Turner, C. S. (2002). *Diversifying the faculty a guidebook for search committees.* Washington, DC: Association of American Colleges.

9 Conclusion
In Solidarity With the Community We Serve

Maria Estela Zarate

Pérez, Arredondo, and López Figueroa (this volume) present figures that plainly illustrate the dire underrepresentation of Chicana and Latina faculty in U.S. colleges and universities. Some have examined the various factors that converge to explain this dismal condition (Myers and Turner, 2004; Turner, González, and Wood, 2008). While all of these factors merit continued examination, it is also vital to continue to consider the ways in which Chicana and Latina faculty experience institutional inclusion and exclusion. To that end, this volume presents individual and collective narratives of persistence and survival in the academy from Chicana and Latina faculty. It is important to document narratives of persistence to enrich our understanding of the challenges faced by Chicanas and Latinas. In addition, personal narratives explain the ways in which the authors contest and survive existing conditions. Given the abysmal underrepresentation of Chicana and Latina faculty, college and university leaders would benefit from reading first-person accounts of how institutional settings hinder or support the professional trajectories of Chicana and Latina faculty.

This concluding chapter aims to first present salient themes and arguments distilled from the previous eight chapters. In particular, I draw attention to the common challenges faced by the authors and the ways in which they navigate and thrive in higher education institutions. I then highlight the frameworks and concepts that the authors have used to capture the lived experiences of Chicana and Latina faculty. Collectively, these frameworks signal the direction in which future scholarship should consider framing the underrepresentation of Chicana and Latina faculty and administrators in academe. I conclude by drawing from the author's narratives to propose recommendations to junior Chicana and Latina faculty and for policy and future research. Finally I offer an appendix with a select list of national resources to find community and support.

In offering these concluding remarks, I follow the authors' approach in rejecting a finite boundary between the personal and the professional and write in the first person. In doing so, I am also signaling how these chapters mirror and reflect my own professional and personal experiences.

I am a first-generation Latina immigrant from a working-class family whose trajectory resembles some aspects of the experiences described by the authors of this volume. Moreover, as a full professor, I am personally and professionally interested in improving the institutional climate facing faculty of color.

Challenges Encountered

As the authors in this volume illustrated, getting a tenure-track job is not the only barrier to greater representation of Chicanas and Latinas in higher-education institutions. After securing a tenure-track position, the pursuit of tenure was a minefield, without trail markers, double standards, and irregular rules of engagement. And even as tenured faculty, Chávez, Herrera, Pérez, Arrendondo, Kiyama, and Gonzales found that career pathways to administration or other leadership positions were riddled with challenges and detractors. In fact, one of the strengths of this volume is the wide range of experiences at different points in an academic career trajectory, from those recently tenured to experienced administrator leaders. And yet the injuries and distractions appear to be constantly present at various points in their academic careers.

In this collection of narratives, injuries, and challenges came from both exclusionary policies and individual detractors who enforced and reproduced broader social hierarchies and dominant narratives. Some injuries derived from broader stereotypes about women and Latinx and Chicanx communities that then permeated interactions and expectations in professional contexts. In Arredondo's experience, "Latina leaders are swept into these broad stereotyped attributes" (p. 110, this volume) of women and expected to perform to the deferential roles assigned to them. Some authors described instances of microaggressions that were ultimately informed by negative stereotypes or deficit views of Chicanx and Latinx communities (Chávez, et al., this volume; Lopez Figueroa, this volume). These instances left authors feeling both dejected and incensed. For some, rejection also came from within the community of Latinx and Chicanx scholars. This is in the case when Chávez et al., described the undermining of their administrative roles by Chicanx male colleagues. This source of injury is often dismissed but important to acknowledge that gendered stereotypes and expectations also surface in Latinx and Chicanx academic communities.

The more common but equally insidious harm resulted from institutionalized practices and policies that, although not explicitly discriminatory, nonetheless neglected obvious disparities in outcomes and representation, normalizing inequities in the institution. In the more innocuous scenarios, policy implementations that lacked transparency brought on distrust of the organization that fed insecurities about accomplishments (Oliva and Nevarez, this volume; Peña, this volume). For first-generation

Chicana and Latina faculty, unclear and nontransparent policies brought about doubts of belonging in the academe. In worse cases, some policies seemingly allowed for inequitable distribution of resources, such as when one new faculty received less start-up funds than another (Oliva and Nevarez, this volume). For some authors, there was sometimes no choice but to challenge unfair policies or treatment at various points in their educational journey (López Figueroa, this volume; Chávez et al., this volume; Vélez and Lees, this volume).

Most narratives described working at institutions that used a discourse of diversity and inclusion but faltered in executing meaningful practices and policies that truly valued inclusion or increased representation of Latinx and Chicanx faculty. Vélez and Lees described having to guard themselves from the exploitation of their bodies as aesthetic representation of diversity and inclusion. At the same time, they experienced rejection and dismissal of their scholarship that addressed exclusion and silencing of marginalized communities. Chávez, Herrera, and Pérez, Peña, and Kiyama and Gonzales all constantly weighed how to be relevant to the institutional goals of diversity and inclusion without having to offer uncompensated labor or be culturally taxed.

Collectively, tenure policies and promotion expectations reflected institutions' assimilationist expectations for Chicana and Latina faculty. Much like broader national politics of belonging and identity, institutions signaled an implicit requirement to assimilate to institutional values of individualism, male-centered inquiry, and self-centered achievement. Expectations of assimilation were evident in the ways Chicana and Latina faculty were expected to interact with others (Arredondo, this volume; Chávez et al., this volume), the ways faculty needed to claim resources (Oliva and Nevarez, this volume) and in tenure standards and expectations (Vélez and Lees, this volume; Oliva and Nevarez, this volume). Despite the multiple barriers that the authors described, the narratives did not reflect submission to institutional values that were culturally incongruous (Oliva and Nevarez, this volume) with the values instilled by their families and communities. Instead the authors offered accounts of survival and strategies for persistence while remaining committed to broader goals of social justice and institutional transformation.

Surviving the Academy Together

The most salient and powerful theme emerging from the previous chapters is the collectivist values of Chicana and Latina faculty. The chapters consistently described their academic careers in the context of service to others and in service to communities. Kiyama and Gonzales described their work as "externally focused" and community centered (p. 35). Others similarly described their community-driven approach to their scholarship, service, and teaching as a "communal approach" (Oliva and Nevarez, this volume, p. 21), "familismo" (Peña, this volume, p. 45), "shared responsibility" (Lopez Figueroa, this volume, p. 63), "in relationship to community/family/land" (Vélez and Lees, this volume, p. 79), or "advocating for our community" (Chávez et al., this volume, p. 98).

For most of the authors and among Arredondo's interviewees, the outward focus on others was grounded in their experience growing up in supportive families and communities. Families and extended communities offered examples of benevolence and communal support, despite community members often facing limited resources themselves. Some also counted teachers, advisors, and university administrators among their community of support. As such, the community-driven approach to their work can be viewed as an extension of their roots and experiences.

The collectivist mind-set of the Chicana and Latina faculty in this volume informed and was informed by broader professional goals of seeking social transformation. In their research and teaching, the authors promoted social justice ideals and transformation. They imagined decolonized institutions that could exist in the service of marginalized communities. The authors asked broader questions about who they serve and in what ways their work advances social justice. Service, in their view, was for the community, not self-serving promotions (Kiyama and Gonzales, this volume). Vélez and Lees questioned and challenged the tenure process that promotes individual scholarship and achievement by reformulating their tenure portfolios to reflect their work and service to the community and commitment to collaboration. This type of activism is perhaps not externally visible but embodied the prominence of collectivist values in their professional lives. That Chicana and Latina faculty resisted dominant standards of individual achievement, in precisely the contexts that seek to erase their presence (Gutiérrez y Muhs, Niemann, Gonzáles, and Harris, 2012), is indeed courageous.

Mentoring Is Critical

Another prominent theme in this volume was the critical role of mentorship in the lives of Chicana and Latina faculty. While various research has documented the importance of mentoring for junior faculty (Sorcinelli and Yun, 2007), less is known about how mentoring varies across cultures, institutions, and tenure rank. This volume illustrated the ways in which Chicana and Latina faculty relied on mentoring in their educational and professional trajectory, while remaining grounded to their community and families. For them, mentoring relationships were not framed in hierarchical and rigid roles where the mentor was the teacher to the mentee. Rather mentoring was positioned as a cycle: we were mentored so we can mentor another and each other. Mentoring was a relationship between advocates for each other. The distinction between "support group" and mentorship was ambiguous. Chicana and Latina faculty are a family that mentors each other, interchanging roles as needed.

The mentoring relationships described in the chapters was unique in the way Chicana and Latina feminist identities were at the center of the mentoring relationships. Oliva and Nevarez discussed how cultural congruency was important between mentor and mentee. Understanding each other's cultural and gendered contexts, beyond the academy, and speaking the same "language" was critical to developing a mentoring relationship. Chávez et al., Vélez and Lees, and Arredondo all used *comadrazgo* to describe the unique bond that defines supportive and mentoring relationships. This collection of narratives demonstrates how in the process of battling and surviving in the academy, an unconditional sisterhood emerged.

One critical element in mentorship and support structures was trust (*confianza*). Trust allowed for genuine relationships where concerns and problems were collectively deliberated. A second critical element in the mentorship relationships was a shared vision of the broader struggle for social justice. Supportive relationships and mentorship were more than tools for achieving the next professional milestone. They were spaces to strategize for a common vision of inclusive higher-education institutions. Finally all the authors described the critical function of mentorship and sisterhood for sharing resources or information that were otherwise inaccessible. They helped each other understand institutions and practices, translating for and guiding each other.

Claiming a space where supportive conversations and mentoring took place was also critical. López Figueroa and Peña both participated in formal and institutionalized mentoring programs to receive and render mentorship and build community. Kiyama and Gonzales relied on an informal network of women of color for support. Chávez et al. intentionally created a Chicana mastermind that met regularly to nurture solidarity, *comadrazgo*, and solve professional dilemmas. They used the lens of *sitios* and *lenguas* (Pérez, 1998) to emphasize the group's function as a Chicana feminist space that "protect[ed] and uplift[ed]" them (Chávez et al., this volume, p. 91). Others relied on both formal and informal spaces to develop supportive relationships. In all spaces, their Chicana and Latina identity and positionality were at the center of the relationships.

A logical extension of their collective tendency to always look outward, to prioritize their community before their career status, was the undertaking of mentoring roles. Supporting similar rank Chicana and Latina faculty and reaching down the tenure-track ladder to hoist others were part of their conceptualization of work. The result was a type of academic kinship, a sisterhood, that transcended generations and rank.

Methodological Considerations

A noteworthy feature of this volume is the use of a wide range of methodological approaches to examining professional experiences, including autoethnography, narrative inquiry, qualitative interviews, and *testimonios*. The methodological variety illustrates the array of standpoints from which we auto-examine diverse experiences. The methodological approaches support the argument that our words, stories, and voices remain the best tools to dismantle the barriers meant to exclude us. We are our own best researchers. In decolonizing the methodologies (Calderón, Delgado Bernal, Perez Huber, Malagón, and Vélez, 2012) that are used to examine the experiences of those in the institutional margins, faculty of color, like those represented in this volume, create an alternate praxis, unbound to the positivist methodological spectrum.

Equally noteworthy was the scope of theoretical and conceptual frameworks used to interpret the experiences of Chicana and Latina faculty. CFE, as a way to capture their "way of moving about and surviving in society" (Kiyama and Gonzales, this volume, p. 32), was the most salient framework. From this theoretical stance, concepts like *nepantla* and *sitios y lenguas* were used to understand specific projects (Arredondo, this volume; Chávez et al., this volume). Using cultural frameworks, Peña argues that *familismo* is a useful concept to understand how she shaped her career. Oliva and Nevarez similarly point to cultural incongruity as the concept that captures the connection or disconnect that first-generation Chicana and Latina faculty encounter as junior faculty. In agreement with the rest of the authors, Arredondo calls for more relevant models of leadership, such as an Indigenous model of leadership. Together, these frameworks demonstrate the importance of situating our narratives in organic theoretical contexts.

Indeed the methodological and theoretical frameworks further underscored how the authors persisted in reclaiming the purpose of their work. They were not singularly driven by ambitions of climbing a tenure ladder and promotions. Rather they were driven by a commitment to advocate for their community, produce scholarship that reflects their community's ways of knowing, nurture future generations, and build academic *familia*.

Recommendations

In the following, I synthesize the recommendations put forth by the authors, according to the audience. While the recommendations do not exhaustively capture the wisdom of the previous chapters, this reference is useful to remind ourselves of what we need to ask from others.

Consejos *for Junior Faculty*

1. Trust the values that you have adopted and/or have been instilled in you. Let these values drive and shape your scholarship, teaching, and service. This way, you can find joy and meaning in your work.
2. Learn to say no when requests are not aligned with your goals and priorities.
3. Invest in creating community and *familia* in and out of the academy. These spaces can be in the institution, the local community, or professional organizations. Create our own mastermind space (Chávez et al., this volume), writing support group, or accountability group to check in and problem-solve issues.
4. Seek mentors and build a network of mentors. Different dimensions of our lives need different types of mentoring so it is important to have more than one mentor. Ask for guidance. If someone turns you down or is not available, move on and seek guidance elsewhere.
5. Take care of your health and your mental well-being (López Figueroa, this volume). You can only take care and advocate for others if you are well.

Building and Nurturing Mentorship

Mentoring and mentorship was critical in the experiences of the authors. Mentors were important to their success, and mentoring remained an important dimension of their service. In seeking mentorship, mentoring others, or building mentoring programs, these are salient features of mentorship described in the volume.

1. A mentor should help the mentee understand the political landscape of the institution, speak the same language as the mentee, and understand intersectional interactions from the mentee's standpoint (Oliva and Nevarez, this volume).
2. At a minimum, mentoring seemed to be more effective when there were cultural congruency and/or relationships were "culturally informed" (Kiyama and Gonzales, this volume, p. 39).
3. Mentorship is most constructive when there is a shared understanding of the values that drive scholarship, teaching, and service. In this volume, successful mentoring was grounded in broader social justice objectives.
4. Mentoring groups or pairs should be done with attention to gender, race, rank, and goals so as to diminish socially imposed barriers.

Institutional Support for Tenure

This volume has stories of feminist empowerment and persistence, informed by unique sources of knowledge and power. Institutions need to recognize and nurture diverse forms and origins of knowledge. Not all faculty subscribe to male-centered and Westernized ways of knowledge production and validation.

1. Institutional standards for tenure need to reflect the fact that, for community-centered scholars, scholarship is often only one aspect of scholars' professional goals. For many scholars, like the authors of this volume, collaboration with and service to the community is a critical element of their professional lives. Thus, tenure and promotion standards need to allow for and validate community-engaged scholarship that seeks impact beyond the top peer-reviewed academic journals.
2. At some institutions, only in-depth, focused bodies of scholarship are validated in tenure reviews. Scholarship that demonstrates breadth of knowledge of the field or shifts in research agendas is often not well-regarded in tenure review. This runs counter to research that is produced for and in the context of social justice goals, where scholarship is often responding to imperative local issues, current political discourse, or individual struggles. Such was the case with Peña when she shifted her research focus to align with her activism around her son's health condition. The result was a richer and more connected research experience, which then yielded remarkable success for Peña and the institution. Tenure standards should not penalize scholars who pivot research agendas mid-course to tenure or promotion.
3. Tenure reviews can reward service that extends beyond formal university committees. Faculty of color often contribute service to the local community and to nurturing safe spaces for underrepresented students and faculty in the university. This type of service is often not included in institutional categories of service. Institutions can explore how faculty can report service outside formal service committees and external to the university in their tenure portfolios.
4. Institutions can provide funding for junior faculty to participate in professional development conferences and programs that support productivity and scholarly engagement. In addition, institutions can fund self-organized support groups to foster community among faculty.
5. Teaching evaluations and assessments can be more comprehensive to account for the different ways that faculty view production and dissemination of knowledge. There is evidence that faculty of color are often unfairly evaluated by students (Smith and Anderson, 2005). While we still have much to learn about how student biases inform their evaluations of instructors, teaching evaluations should consider and capture the different ways that faculty interact with students, build community in the classroom, and value different sources of knowledge.

Institutional Culture

1. In Chapter 4, Peña uses the term *intentionality* to describe how the provost at her institution sought to increase Latinx tenure-track faculty at the university. The argument is that if institutions want to shift organization culture to support faculty of color, then leaders and administrators need to demonstrate their commitment in the way resources are distributed, goals are prioritized, and policies are implemented.
2. Given the underrepresentation of faculty of color at most colleges and universities, institutions should invest in developing faculty allies to support and engage in diversity, equity, and inclusion initiatives. In this way, faculty of color do not become unfairly burdened with service demands. Of course, faculty who serve in this capacity should be adequately compensated as well.
3. Some of the authors in this volume who are full professors implicitly and directly pose the question, "Now what?" Institutions should enable this talent and invest in providing leadership development opportunities for faculty of color. Chávez et al. suggest investing in developing cohorts of women of color that include mentors and support for leadership positions. This may involve funding professional development opportunities in national conferences and programs that support women of color faculty and leaders.

References

Calderón, D., Delgado Bernal, D., Perez Huber, L., Malagón, M., and Vélez, V. N. (2012). A Chicana feminist epistemology revisited: Cultivating ideas a generation later. *Harvard Educational Review*, 82(4), 513–540.

Gutiérrez y Muhs, G., Niemann, Y. F, Gonzáles, C. G., and Harris, A. P. (2012). *Presumed incompetent: The intersections of race and class for women in academia*. Boulder, CO: University Press of Colorado.

Myers, Jr. S. L., and Turner, C. S. (2004). The effects of Ph.D. supply on minority faculty representation. *American Economic Review*, 94(2), 296–301.

Pérez, E. (1998). Irigaray's female symbolic in the making of Chicana lesbian *sitios y lenguas* (Sites and Discourses). In C. Trujillo (Ed.), *Living Chicana theory* (pp. 87–101). Berkeley, CA: Third Woman Press.

Smith, G., and Anderson, K. J. (2005). Students' ratings of professors: The teaching style contingency for Latino/a professors. *Journal of Latinos and Education*, 4(2), 115–136.

Sorcinelli, M. D., and Yun, J. (2007). From mentor to mentoring networks: Mentoring in the new academy. *Change: The Magazine of Higher Learning*, 39, 58–61.

Turner, C. S. V., González, J. C., and Wood, J. L. (2008). Faculty of color in academe: What 20 years of literature tells us. *Journal of Diversity in Higher Education*, 1(3), 139–168.

Appendix A
Resources for Building Community and Seeking Support

American Association of Hispanics in Higher Education (ahhee.org)—AAHHE has several funded programs to support junior faculty and graduate students. More recently, they have instituted a Leadership Academy Fellows program to support leadership development.

Faculty Women of Color in the Academy (cpe.vt.edu/fwca)—FWCA provides an annual conference for university administrators, faculty, graduate students, and post-docs offering a "unique" opportunity to "network and engage with peers from around the country."

HERS Institute: Higher Education Leadership Development Program (https://www.hersnetwork.org/programs/hers-institute/)—This intensive multi-day leadership development program targets women (and all who identify as women) who are on an administrator career path. Ideal candidates are in mid- to senior-level positions in higher education organizations.

Hispanic Association of Colleges and Universities (hacu.net)—HACU hosts an annual conference where student success programs are highlighted. There is also the Latino Higher Education Leadership Institute as a pre-conference event.

Keeping Our Faculty of Color Conference (idea.umn.edu/symposia/keeping-our-faculty)—This annual conference hosted by the Institute for Diversity, Equity, and Advocacy at the University of Minnesota has the objective of promoting faculty diversity.

Mujeres Activas en Letras y Cambio Social (malcs.org)—MALCS fosters a community of Chicana, Latina, Native American, and gender nonconforming students and faculty in academe. They host a summer institute and publish a peer-reviewed journal.

National Center for Faculty Diversity and Development (facultydiversity.org)—NCFDD provides professional development programs to support faculty, administrators, post-docs, and graduate students. Their keystone program is a writing boot camp called the Faculty Success Program, a twelve-week program where a coach leads small groups through evidence-based strategies to increase productivity while maintaining work-life balance. Some faculty are able to use their start-up or professional development funds to become a member of the center or participate in one of their programs.

Select Volumes with Personal Accounts of Surviving in the Academy

Castellanos, J., Gloria, A., and Kamimura, M. (2006). *The Latina/o pathway to the Ph.D: Abriendo caminos.* Sterling, VA: Stylus Publishing, LLC.

Gutiérrez y Muhs, G., Flores Niemann, Y., Gonzalez, C., and Harris, A. (2012). *Presumed incompetent: The intersections of race and class for women in academia.* Boulder, CO: University of Colorado Press.

The Latina Feminist Group. (2001). *Telling to live: Latina feminist testimonios.* Durham, NC: Duke University Press.

Santamaría, L. J., Jean-Marie, G., and Grant, C. M. (2014). *Cross-cultural women scholars in academe: Intergenerational voices.* New York, NY: Routledge.

Stanley, C. (2006). *Faculty of color: Teaching in predominantly White colleges and universities.* Bolton, MA: Anker Publishing Company.

Whitaker, M. C., and Grollman, E. A. (2019). *Counternarratives from women of color academics: Bravery, vulnerability, and resistance.* New York, NY: Routledge.

Contributors

Patricia Arredondo, EdD, NCC has had a successful career as senior administrator in higher education, tenured full professor, organizational consultant, and professional organization leader. She is the first Latina to serve as president of the American Counseling Association (ACA) (2005–2006). Patricia has been an ACA "activist" as founding member of the Counselor for Social Justice and the Women's Interest and Mentoring Network. She holds fellow status with ACA and the American Psychological Association. She is the founding president of the National Latinx Psychological Association. Dr. Arredondo holds a BA degree from Kent State in Spanish and journalism, a MA in counseling from Boston College, and an EdD from Boston University in counseling psychology. She is a licensed psychologist and National Certified Counselor. She is president of the Arredondo Advisory Group. Originally from Lorain, Ohio, she currently resides in Phoenix, Arizona.

Marisela R. Chávez, PhD is associate professor and current chair of Chicana and Chicano studies at California State University, Dominguez Hills. She received her PhD in history from Stanford University and has published articles on Chicana feminist history in *Chicana Movidas: New Narratives of Activism and Feminism in the Movement Era* (University of Texas Press, 2018), *No Permanent Waves: Recasting U.S. Feminist History* (Rutgers University Press, 2010), and *Memories and Migrations: Mapping Boricua and Chicana Histories* (University of Illinois Press, 2008). Presently she is revising a manuscript that traces Chicana and Mexican American women's activism in Los Angeles from the 1960s to 1980.

Leslie Gonzales, PhD is an associate professor of higher, adult and lifelong education at Michigan State University. Gonzales's research agenda consists of three overarching lines of inquiry: legitimacy within the academic profession and the broader field of higher education; relations of power that govern the recognition of knowledge and knowers; and the possibility of agency among academics to negotiate, remake, or resist marginalizing structural and cultural features of academia. Gonzales is a Latina, working-class, first-generation college student-turned-academic and earned all three academic degrees from HSIs, including New Mexico Highlands University and the University of Texas at El Paso.

Cristina Herrera, PhD earned her doctorate in English from Claremont Graduate University and is professor and chair of Chicano and Latin American studies at California State University, Fresno. She is the author of the 2014 study *Contemporary Chicana Literature: (Re)Writing the Maternal Script*, and has co-edited multiple books on Latinx literature, including the first book-length volume on Chican@ children's literature, *Voices of Resistance: Interdisciplinary Approaches to Chican@ Children's Literature* (with Laura Alamillo and Larissa Mercado-López, 2017). Cristina has published articles in *Chicana/Latina Studies*, *Women's Studies: An Interdisciplinary Journal*, *Critique: Studies in Contemporary Fiction*, *Children's Literature*, and other journals. She is currently working on a number of projects related to Chicana and Latina young adult literature.

Anna Lees, EdD (Little Traverse Bay Band of Odawa Indians, descendant) began her career as an early childhood classroom teacher in rural northern Michigan. Now an assistant professor of early childhood education in Woodring College of Education at Western Washington University, she partners with schools and communities to prepare teachers for the holistic needs of children, families, and communities. Anna is committed to developing and sustaining reciprocal relationships with Indigenous communities to engage community leaders as co-teacher educators, opening spaces for Indigenous epistemologies in early childhood settings and higher education. Anna advocates for intergenerational and land-based relationships in educational settings, believing that decolonizing interactions with young children will begin the path toward a postcolonial future.

Julie López Figueroa, PhD is a professor of ethnic studies at Sacramento State University. With a focus on retention, her qualitative research focuses on access and success of first-generation college students within higher education, specifically Latino males. She is nationally recognized as one of the earliest contributors informing and framing the body of knowledge examining the academic success of Latino males in higher education. Julie completed her doctoral studies in education from the University of California, Berkeley; her MA in education from the University of California, Santa Cruz; and her BA in sociology and Chicano studies from the University of California, Davis. She's the proud daughter of Mexican migrant parents, Macedonio and Maria Figueroa.

Judy Marquez Kiyama, PhD is an associate professor and chair in the higher education department at the University of Denver's Morgridge College of Education. Kiyama's research examines the structures that shape educational opportunities for underserved groups through an asset-based lens to better understand the collective knowledge and resources drawn upon to confront, negotiate, and (re)shape such structures. Kiyama grounds her work in community knowledge and organizes her research in three interconnected areas: the role of parents and families; equity and power in educational research; and underserved groups as collective networks of change. As a first-generation Mexican American college student, Dr. Kiyama draws on her own experiences with her family to connect with the sources of support that first-generation families of color offer their students in the transition to college.

Lucinda Nevarez, PhD is a master's level social worker who has been a member of the Department of Social Work at the University of Texas at San Antonio (UTSA) since 2013. Her areas of scholarly interest include health disparities and inequalities, minority health and mental health issues, health policy, and healthcare access and utilization. This work includes a focus on the influence of race and culture in accessing and the utilization of mental health and healthcare services. Dr. Nevarez was recognized as Professor of the Year by the Department of Social Work and College of Public Policy at UTSA in 2016. She is a former Kellogg Health Scholar and served as a fellow in the Kaiser Permanente Burch Minority Leadership Development Program.

Maricela Oliva, PhD is associate dean for faculty development and associate professor for the higher education program in the College of Education and Human Development at the University of Texas at San Antonio. She has served professional associations like the American Educational Research Association, the Association for the Study of Higher Education, and the American Association of Hispanics in Higher Education through conference planning, nominating, evaluation, awards, and training committees. She serves on numerous editorial boards. Her professional and organizational leadership has been recognized by the 2008 University of Texas at San Antonio President's Distinguished Achievement Award for Excellence in University Service, the 2011 Diane Abdo Outstanding Organizational Advisor Award, the 2012 Faculty Member of the Year for the Texas Association of College and University Student Personnel Administrators, the 2016 Distinguished University Faculty for the Texas Association of Chicanos in Higher Education, and the 2018 Women's Leadership Award. Her areas of research interest include Latino/underrepresented student college access, P-20 (school-university collaboration), cross-cultural issues in higher education, higher education policy, and faculty mentoring.

Edlyn Peña, PhD is an associate professor of higher education leadership and director of the Autism and Communication Center (ACC) at California Lutheran University. She began her research career exploring how faculty members can improve their teaching and advising practices with Latinx and African American college students. When her son was diagnosed with autism in 2010, Dr. Peña pivoted her research agenda toward understanding ways in which to support college students with disabilities, particularly autism. The aim of her scholarship and advocacy is to empower students with disabilities from historically marginalized backgrounds to achieve equitable access and outcomes in higher education. In Dr. Peña's award-winning research, she examines these critical issues from the lenses of social justice, intersectionality, and neurodiversity. As the director of the ACC and member of the federal Interagency Autism Coordinating Committee, Dr. Peña is best known for her service to the autism community at state and national levels.

Patricia A. Pérez, PhD is a professor and chair of Chicana/o studies at California State University, Fullerton. Her research focuses on postsecondary equity and equality of opportunity for Latina/o and im/migrant students. Dr. Pérez is the co-editor of *Higher Education Access and Choice for Latino Students: Critical Findings and Theoretical Perspectives* and *Facilitating Educational Success for Migrant Farmworker Students in the U.S.*, both published by Routledge. Dr. Pérez received an MA and PhD from the UCLA Graduate School of Education and Information Studies. She also holds an EdM with a concentration in administration, planning, and social policy from Harvard University and a BA from UCLA in Chicana/o Studies. She is the recipient of several awards, including recognition for exceptional teaching, service, scholarship, and honors for outstanding mentorship.

Caroline S. Turner, PhD is professor, doctorate in educational leadership, California State University, Sacramento, and Lincoln Professor Emerita, higher and postsecondary education, Arizona State University. She also served as president of the Association for the Study of Higher Education (ASHE). Recognizing her exemplary scholarship, Turner is the 2009 recipient of the American Educational Research Association (AERA) Scholars of Color in Education Distinguished Career Contribution Award, the 2009 AERA Dr. Carlos J. Vallejo Memorial Award for Lifetime Scholarship, and the 2008 Recipient of the ASHE Council on Ethnic Participation Mildred Garcia Award for Exemplary Scholarship. Recently she was named a Distinguished Alumni Scholar by Stanford University and presented with the 2016 University of California, Davis (UCD) School of Education Distinguished Alumni Award. In 2018, she was invited to present the commencement address for the UCD School of Education. Turner received her BA in history and MA in educational psychology from the University of California, Davis. She received her PhD in administration and policy analysis from the Stanford University School of Education.

Verónica N. Vélez, PhD is an associate professor and founding director of the education and social justice minor at Western Washington University. Her research focuses on migrant mother activism, community-based participatory action research in grassroots contexts, popular education, and the use of digital mapping technologies to explore the spatial dimensions of educational (in)opportunity. Each of these areas is informed by her interdisciplinary training and expertise in critical race theory (CRT), Latinx/a/o critical theory (LatCrit), radical cartography, and Chicana feminist epistemologies (CFE). She has published in multiple academic journals including *Educational Foundations*, *Harvard Educational Review*, *Association of Mexican American Educators Journal*, and *Race, Ethnicity, and Education*, in addition to several chapters in edited anthologies. She completed an MA and PhD in education from UCLA with a specialization in race and ethnic studies and a BA in psychology from Stanford University.

Maria Estela Zarate, PhD is professor in the Department of Educational Leadership at California State University, Fullerton, where she teaches future education leaders. Her research publications address the trajectory of immigrant students in U.S. schools, including the connections between schools and families. In 2017, she co-edited a volume on educational interventions for migrant students. More recently, she has examined dual language programs, including state policy, and organization and leadership challenges in such programs.

Index

academia ix–x, 1–8, 19, 21–25, 75; being Latina 52, 57, 67, 69, 99, 104; challenges to 39; service in *see* service; and working-class communities 37
Acevedo-Gil, Nancy 11, 12, 67
activism 53, 73, 133, 137, 141, 145
adversity 108, 114, 116, 118, 123–124, 126
Aleman, Enrique 67
American Association of Hispanics in Higher Education (AAHHE) 109
American Association of University Presidents (AAUP) 108
Anishinaabemowin 77
Anzaldúa, Gloria 7, 106, 108, 112
Arredondo, Patricia 7, 106–129, 130–135, 141
Association for the Study of Higher Education (ASHE) x, xi, 11, 43
autism 46, 53, 54, 144
Autism and Communication Center (ACC) 53
autoethnography 44, 45, 135

Baquedano-Lopez, Patricia 67
Bautista Pertuz, Sofia 5, 6
Beauvoir, Simone de 108
Bensimon, Estela 67
Berta-Avila, Margarita 67
bicultural identity 108, 115, 116
Blackwell, Maylei 91
'borderlands' 5, 7, 106; context for Latina leaders 107–108; experiences of 115; navigating 113–114
boundary crosser 108
Brazil-Cruz, Lisceth 67
Burciaga, Rebeca 67

Castellanos, Jeanett 67
Castro-Villareal, Felicia 5
change agents 3, 66
Chávez, César 118
Chávez, Marisela R. 7, 90–105, 112, 131–136, 138, 141
Chicana and Latina faculty in higher education ix–xi, 1–8, 56, 63, 65, 74; claiming space 100–101; collective narratives 94–98; creating *confianza* 101–102; intersectionality 90; leadership *see* Chicana leadership; personal stories 91–94; triumphs of 98–100; sharing and mentorship 102–103; *see also* Latina faculty
Chicana department chairs 7, 40, 52, 90, 91, 99–104, 108, 115; challenges to 94–98
Chicana feminism 7, 31–33, 40, 75, 78, 82; testimonial practices 90–91, 135, 145
Chicana feminist epistemology (CFE) 7, 31, 32–33, 75, 82, 85, 135, 142, 145
Chicana leadership ix–xi, 6, 7, 19, 27, 34–36, 122–124; in the Academy 90; culture-centered approaches 113–118; managing and navigating 100–102; organizational change 44; paradigms 111–113; practical and policy implications 102–104; sexist challenges to 49; styles 52; supporting promotion of Latina faculty through 45
Chicana Mastermind xii, 7, 90, 99, 100–102, 134, 136
Chicana/o Studies 63, 71; and ethnic studies departments 90, 100
Chicanx 105n2

collective approach and mindset 15, 18, 117, 124, 133, 134
collective method 4, 114
colonialism 75, 77, 78, 81; anti-colonial 79; post-colonial 73, 76, 80, 86, 142; settler-colonialism 75, 81, 85
comadrazgo (academic kin) 7, 100, 101–102, 134
comadre 73, 76–79, 85, 100, 117; definition of 86n1
community/family/land 79, 133
community-driven 35, 132, 133; community before career 134
confianza 7, 100, 101–102, 134; definition of 86n1
consejos for junior faculty 136–138
Contreras, Frances 67
coraje 125
counter-spaces of cultural citizenship 39
courage 40, 48, 114, 116–118, 133
Cox, M. 5
critical race theory 4, 5, 145
Cuellar, Marcela 67
Cueva, Berta 4–5
cultural taxation 47–48

decolonized, decolonization 73, 79, 80, 81, 142; curriculum 83; methodologies 135; spaces 91, 133
Delgado Bernal, D. 32
deliberateness 116–118, 126
desafios 127
dichos 116, 125
diversity: activism 74; approaches to 27; disputed 26; epistemological 86; committees 47; concerns 17; incorporating 28; faculty x, 2, 118–119, 121; hiring 44; of Latina ethnic representation 8; mentoring 48; and organizational change 51, 52; of perspectives 24; pitfalls 84; roles 5; stereotypes 127; of thought 15; training 6; voice of 107; work 37
Dyson, Anne Hass 63

early socialization *see* socialization
educational scholars 79
emotional intelligence (EI) 7, 112–113, 124; four domains of 112
empathy 112, 113
ethnic stereotypes 3, 109, 110, 111, 114, 116, 127

ethnic studies 93, 94, 95, 97–98, 100
Eurocentric leadership models 112

Facio, Elisa 71
Facio, Linda 67
faculty programming and development i, 2, 6, 12, 18, 39, 41; institutional 102–103, 118, 119; and mentoring 65, 66, 68; space for 100; for tenure 50–53, 56; 74, 85
familismo 7, 34, 45–47, 51, 133
familias 125
family x–xi, 5, 15, 19, 21; being far from 36; Chicana and Latina faculty as a 134; experiences 33, 57, 58, 59, 131, 134; expectations 92; extended 91; first 47; importance of 75, 79; lessons 38; loyalty 46, 106; as mentors and role models 22, 24, 37, 106, 116, 117; money 34; obligations 6, 93, 101, 104; resource 115; values 52; and work balance 45, 48, 64, 100
Flores, Yvette 67
"from the fringe" 78

Garcia, Eugene 64
gender xi, 3, 5, 15–16, 27, 28; behaviors 110; binary 77; contexts 134; exclusion based on 109; expectations 92, 131; fluid 87n7; gendered organizations 45, 48; identity 113; institutional gender dynamics 51; non-conforming 87n7, 139; norms 91
Gonzales, Leslie x, 6, 31–43, 131, 132–136, 141
gratitude 57, 67–68, 142

Harper, Shaun 67
Herrera, Cristina, 40, 90–105, 131, 132, 142
heteropatriarchy 77, 78, 109
heterosexism 109
historically underserved communities 32, 37, 38, 53, 121
hostile work environments 6, 15, 28, 66, 91, 117
Hurtado, Aída 63, 64, 67

identity: barriers due to 26; crossing boundaries of 112; ethnocultural 20, 22, 106, 107; gendered 77, 113; as a Latina 27, 108, 114, 125–126, 132–134; status 111

inclusion 17, 21, 37, 53, 73, 99, 107, 130
indigenous: children and families 81; communities 74, 85; education 80; epistemologies 7, 75; faculty 79, 86; leadership models 112; scholars 73; self 107
Indigenous Studies 74
individualism 21, 56, 79, 132
institutional structures and policy *see* postsecondary institutional structures
intentionality ix, 2, 7, 44, 47, 57, 63; and diversity 118, 138n1; gender and race 103; institutional 51; and m(othering) 84, 85
intergenerational dreams of the postcolonial 7, 73, 85–86
intergenerational kin 46
intergenerational mentorship i, 2, 73, 77, 83, 84; *see also* mentoring
isolation 5, 20–23, 27, 66; 68, 103

junior faculty 15–18, 22, 26–27, 52, 56–57; mentorship 67–68, 133, 135–137; resources for 139

kinship 101, 134
Kiyama, Judy Marquez x, 6, 31–43, 131, 132–136, 141
kwe 77, 78

Ladson-Billings, Gloria 67
Latina administrators x–xi, 2–8, 40–41, 47, 99; most/least gratifying experiences of 118–122; being a *neplantlera* 108; *see also* Chicana department chairs; Chicana leadership; resonant leadership
Latina identity *see* identity
Latina faculty ix–xi, 1–8; cultural practice of being 57; diversity 118–120; in engineering 5; finding voice 11–28; institutional supports for 49–51; intersectional discussion of 90; recruitment and retention 44–45, 52–53; role models 94; and service demands 31–32, 39–41; underrepresentation of 130
Latinx 91, 132; definition of 105n2; Latinx/Chicanx communities 74, 85; stereotypes 131
Latinx/a/o critical theory (LatCrit) 145

Latinx students 28, 49–50, 52–53, 74, 107, 119; increasing numbers of 1, 3, 8, 28; marginalization of 4, 5, 13–14, 23, 121
Lees, Anna x, 7, 73–89, 132–135, 142
lengua 91 *see also sitios y lenguas*
López Figueroa, Julie x, 7, 56–72, 130–134, 136, 142
Luna, G. 5, 6

Madrigal-Garcia, Yanira 11, 12, 67
mandamientos 114
marginalization x, 5, 77
Maria Paradox, The 114
Martinez, Danny 67
McGee, E. 5
Medina, C. 5, 6
mentoring, mentorship ix, 6, 7, 11, 57, 63; among women of color 39, 41, 50, 63, 66; critical role of 133–134; as a cycle 133; by faculty of color 47, 50, 68, 74, 77, 83, 98; lack of 4, 18; models for 23; networks 136; programs 12, 18, 52, 103; relationships 23–28, 133; by senior faculty 67; sharing and 102; contributing to tenure 83, 85; *see also* junior faculty
mestiza 107
Mexican American: activism 141; community 14; families 61; first generation 143; migrant and immigrants 58, 142; socialization 106; students 33, 35; university leaders 115
Mexican American Legal Defense and Education Fund (MALDEF) 13
microaggressions 5, 15, 92, 107, 110, 118; managing 114, 123–124, 131
migrant mother activism 145
Minority Undergraduate Researchers in Letters and Science (MURALS) 62, 63
'mother' 77
m(other), m(othering) 73, 77, 78; knowledge 80; movements 83–85; space/place 80, 83
M(other)work as Radical Resurgence 76–86
mujerista 107
multicultural counseling 112, 113, 115

Nahuatl 135
narrative inquiry 135
National Center for Faculty Development and Diversity 102–103
neoliberalism 73, 75, 77, 98; institutional 79, 80; university 102, 104
nepantla, nepantlera 7, 108, 112, 135
Nevarez, Lucinda 4, 6, 11–30, 132, 133; and mentorship 18, 134, 135
"niceness" 11
Noguera, Pedro 63, 67

Okhremtchouck, Irina 67
Oliva, Maricela 4, 6, 11–30, 132, 133; and mentorship 18, 134, 135
Omi, Michael 63, 67
Optimal Learning Environment Project (O.L.E) 62, 63
Osah Gan Gio model 112
otherness 108; *see also* m(othering)

Papalewis, Rosemary 64
patriarchy 32, 37, 78, 102, 104, 109
peer support 67
Peña, Edlyn 6–7, 44–55, 131–135, 137, 138, 144
Pérez, Emma 91
Pérez, Patricia A. x, 1–10, 67, 90–105, 130–134, 144
Pequera, Beatriz 67
Pizarro, Marcos 67
Ponjuan, Luis 1, 67
postsecondary institutional structures and policies 2, 7, 8, 15, 38; clashes with 127; and equity advocates 47; inclusion and exclusion 130; and intentionality *see* intentionality; preserving white supremacy 74–78, 83; regarding tenure 20, 21, 26, 45; revised to support Chicana faculty 90, 107, 118; shortcomings 120; supporting Latinx students 49–51
positionality 77, 79, 134
predominantly white institutions (PWI) 106, 108, 110, 114, 115, 119, 122
Presumed Incompetent 9, 31
Puertorriqueña 125
Puerto Rican heritage 108, 109, 115, 146

qualitative research 2, 3, 5; interviews 135
Quijada, Patricia 67

racial inequality 66
race/ethnicity and gender xi, 48, 103, 136
"race card" 125
radical 78, 84
Radical Resurgence *see* M(other)work as Radical Resurgence
Radical Resurgence Project 86
reciprocity 57, 67–68, 142
relationship management 112
remediation 123
Rendon, Laura 64
research, teaching, and service 78, 80, 86, 132, 136
resisting and persisting x, 6, 31, 57
resonant leadership 7, 106, 113, 126–127
respeto al projimo 117, 119
Rodriguez, Francisco 64
Rodriguez, Gloria M. 67, 68, 69
Rodríguez, James 67
Rolle, Anthony 67
Ruiz, Vicki 67

sabotage 96, 122, 123, 126
Saenz, Victor 67
Saldaña, L.P. 5
Sambamurthy, N. 5
Sanchez, Patricia 67
Sanchez-Peña, M. 5
self-awareness 112
self-care ix, 104, 124
self-management 112
self-promotion 56
service and service loads ix, 5, 6, 16, 20, 23, 31–41; demands made regarding 47–48, 57, 76, 137, 138; obligation to perform 81; requests 84; requirements 83; scholarship and 68, 82; standards of 65; and tenure 64, 69, 70, 85, 135
settler-colonialism *see* colonialism
"shared responsibility" 133
Simpson, L.B. 75, 76, 77, 78
sisterhood 7, 73, 74, 79; and m(other) work 77, 84, 85
sitios 91, 134
sitios y lenguas (spaces and languages) 7, 90–91, 134, 135

survival in the academy i, 2, 130, 132
social awareness 112
social justice 52, 63, 65, 73, 82, 84, 94; commitment to 74, 99; goals of 132, 137; mentoring and 136; and social transformation 133; struggle for 134; teaching for 83
social reproduction 56
socialization i, 2, 11–14, 27, 46, 106
solidarity 4, 35, 75, 91, 94, 100
Solorzano, Daniel 64, 67, 68
Sosa, E. 5
Sotelo Turner, Caroline 64
Stoner, Mark 64
"subversive" 99
support networks 1, 4, 7, 10, 25, 57, 127; lack of 19, 21, 22; peer support 66, 67

teaching 4, 5, 23; and advising 83; evaluations 76; heavy teaching loads 34; *see* research, teaching, and service
Ten Commandments of Marianismo 114, 117
tenure and promotion for women faculty of color 1–8; challenges 131–132; criteria 68; expectations 19, 28, 76, 125, 132; files 81, 83; guiding principles to achieve 69–71; importance of knowledge about 20, 21; institutionalized support for 49–53, 136–138; ladder 135; mentoring 12, 25, 28, 65, 134; navigating 26, 73, 76; personal experiences 45; process 46, 56, 64, 69, 78, 84, 133; post-tenure 32–39, 53–54; review 57, 60, 64, 66–67, 79, 80, 82; successful tenure 18, 31, 44, 86, 90, 99; tenure-track 74, 75, 85, 93, 96, 98, 122; systemic challenges 20–23, 44; timeline 46–47; *see also* untenured faculty of color
Tellez, Michelle 78
testimonio 4–5, 73, 87n4, 112, 113, 114, 135
tokenism 5
triunfos y tribulaciones (triumphs and challenges) 7, 90
Turner, Caroline Sotelo ix–xi, xii, 4, 64, 67, 73, 130, 144

underrepresentation 56, 130, 137, 138
unprofessional 83, 95, 97
untenured faculty of color 16, 50; *see also* junior faculty

Valenzuela, Angela 67
Vélez, Verónica x, 7, 31, 67, 73–89, 132–135, 145
visible racial ethnic group (VERG) 107

warriors 1, 3
"ways of knowing" 113
"white fragility" 124
white privilege 64, 111
whiteness 32, 77, 109; and niceness 110–111
wild zone metaphor 107

Yosso, Tara 67

Zarate, Maria Estela 7–8, 130–138, 144